NK

€19.95

HOME

THE
BICHON FRISE
TODAY

Jackie Ransom

RINGPRESS

Published by Ringpress Books Ltd,
PO Box 8, Lydney, Gloucestershire GL15 4YN

Designed by Rob Benson

First Published 1999
© 1999 RINGPRESS BOOKS

ISBN 1 86054 131 3

Printed and bound in Singapore
by Kyodo Printing Co

10 9 8 7 6 5 4 3 2 1

Photo: Marc Henrie.

CONTENTS

PREFACE

There is sorrow enough the natural way From men and women to fill our day; And when we are certain of sorry in store, Why do we always arrange for more? Brothers and sisters, I beg you beware Of giving your heart to a dog to tear.

THE POWER OF THE DOG
R. Kipling.

When reading this book about such a charming breed as the Bichon Frisé, please do realise that the Bichon, as we know it today, is a relative newcomer. The Bichon history in this book bears little resemblance to the well-documented histories, going back for hundreds of years, which you will find in the books written about the long-established breeds recognised by the KC and the AKC. The Bichon Frisé does not, as yet, have any history of consequence. The Bichon breed has been mentioned in literature for over two centuries, and small white dogs have been known to exist in various parts of the world long before that, but our Bichon Frisé was identified relatively recently, with its country of origin given as Belgium.

The breed became far too commercially popular from the very first time it was seen in the show ring. The first Bichon arrived in the UK in 1974 and registrations in that year were just six. Only five years later this number had risen to 354. This rapid expansion was the result of too much haphazard breeding by many people for whom the Bichon became the first dog they had owned and this was their first experience of the dog scene in general.

Ignorance is not always bliss, especially when dealing with the breeding of livestock.

Although I had pleasure in breeding and exhibiting both Miniature and Toy Poodles for many years, the pleasure and joy afforded me by my many

A typical Bichon greeting – this is a unique breed characteristic.

Bichon companions, both in the show ring and at home, cannot be expressed in words; it is a delightful breed.

This little French description of the Bichon, given to me by a French breeder in 1974, sums up the Bichon's head and expression to perfection.

Deux boutons de bottine = two boot buttons = the Bichon's round dark eyes.

Un morceau de charbon = a morsel of carbon = their black shiny noses.

Le visage enfariné = the floured face = their white-coated faces.

Je suis clown = I am a clown = the Bichon's amusing antics.

I hope this book will be of interest, as well as an assistance, to owners and to the many other breeders and devotees of the Bichon Frisé. I would also like to thank my son Stuart for his encouragement and help in writing it.

INTRODUCTION

It does not seem possible that 24 years have passed since, for the first time, I saw a live Bichon Frisé. I had seen many illustrations in various magazines but to see a litter of Bichon puppies running around was a revelation.

I became quite enchanted with the breed. The adults and puppies had such charming temperaments, and their beautiful white curly coats, their dark sparkling eyes and their melting expression I found irresistible. Without hesitation I chose two delightful puppies to come and live with my silver Poodles. They were Carlise Cicero of Tresilva, who became an Australian Champion, and Carlise Circe, a bitch puppy who lived with us until she died in 1985.

At that time, as the Bichon on the Continent was always shown untrimmed, I thought how much easier and more pleasant it would be to own a glamorous-coated breed, without the necessity of the endless preparation all Poodle varieties require.

I had been breeding and exhibiting Miniature and Toy Poodles for 14 years, and in order to exhibit a Poodle in the Lion Clip, which at that time was compulsory in the show ring for all Poodles, grooming required the use of clippers and scissors which took so much time and energy. I really thought the Bichon would be much easier to present – I was soon to be proved wrong.

Because the breed was in its infancy, certainly as far as the UK was concerned, I also thought it probable that anyone becoming interested in the breed would realise that we would be in a position to breed sound and healthy specimens, especially if we made certain that we were careful to import only Bichons of top quality, completely free of any hereditary faults.

It did not take me very long to realise that, of the two puppies that I had bought, the bitch puppy, Carlise Circe, did not conform to my idea of a first-class Bichon. Her proportions were vastly different to those required in the

Standard; she had very solid bones, her back was too long and she had rather a light eye.

In my opinion, all bitches used for breeding should, as near as possible, conform to the Breed Standard. To start any breeding programme with a bitch lacking in breed type would be a waste of time and money, so I decided to import a dog and a bitch from the breed's country of origin, Belgium.

After visiting many shows and kennels in France and Belgium I found, and imported in May 1975, two very promising puppies from the Continent.

The bitch, Zena de Chaponay of Tresilva, was so very lovely in appearance, winning no less than 14 Firsts and 12 BOBs, four of these at Championship Shows (the breed was not allocated Challenge Certificates in those days). The dog was Zethus de Chaponay of Tresilva. Although he won a First at Richmond Championship Show in 1975 he really did not like the show ring; the six months in quarantine had taken its toll.

However, this dog was worth his weight in gold as a sire. He had a fabulous head and eye, and firm unbroken pigmentation, with good overall conformation. He was sired by Bel. Int. Ch. Xorba de Chaponay. Zethus de Chaponay of Tresilva sired my first Champion, Ch. Gosmore Tresilva Zorba. At the very first Show

A head study of Zena de Chaponay of Tresilva. Note the attractive long ear fringes

Photo: Marc Henrie.

9

Zethus and Zena de Chaponay of Tresilva: The first Belgian Bichons imported into the UK.

with CCs on offer for the Bichons, Crufts 1980, with Mr Lionel Hamilton Renwick judging, Zorba won the Dog CC, BOB and was a finalist in the Toy Group. Zorba became the first home-bred Champion in the UK. All my Tresilva English Champions have been and still are line-bred back to Zethus.

The Bichon's natural coat with its lovely soft, curly texture is so beautiful it would be a tragedy if, by heavy trimming, the loose silky curls were cut off.

I did expect that we would keep the coat in its natural curl, only trimming the hair to tidy the face and head, the outline of the body, and the legs and feet. This would have rendered the Bichon's trim similar to that of the Soft-Coated Wheaten Terrier, a breed where over-trimming is penalised, but the Wheaten's soft, silky coat may be tidied to present a neat outline.

This natural presentation for the Bichon I really thought would become accepted, especially as both the original FCI Standard of 1933 and the one issued by the FCI in 1972 stated: "the dog may be presented untrimmed or have muzzle and feet slightly tidied up." This clause still appears in the English Breed Standard today but is completely ignored by both exhibitors and judges.

There was one other clause in the original French Standard and in the Kennel Club's Interim Standard issued in 1976 which I had hoped would be retained; this was the clause "smallness being highly desirable". After all, the Bichon is considered a Toy breed in the UK; but others thought differently.

Zena De Chaponay of Tresilva in natural coat.

I expect the clause regarding trimming will be altered by the KC in the near future, as all Bichons seen in the ring today are always presented heavily trimmed in the American style.

There have been a few changes in the Bichon scene. Most of the first UK breeders have left but as the breed continues to rise in popularity we have many new devotees.

Happily one important feature has not changed. The breed still has the gentle, kind, affectionate and amusing temperament today that I found in 1974.

Although various books on the Bichon Frisé have been written in the USA, the first to be written on the breed in the UK was published in 1978.

Twenty years on I have, in this book, included new facts and information which I hope will be of interest to all Bichon devotees.

1 *HISTORY OF THE BREED*

The Bichon Frisé is a very beautiful dog, with a most appealing head and expression. It is small in size but sturdy, and possesses a charming and amusing temperament. Therefore, as the Bichon, as a breed, appears to have been known for many years, being very much in vogue in England, France, Holland and Spain in the 18th century, I find it hard to understand why there are so few references to the Bichon Ténériffe or to the Canary Island's Bichon in any of the books written in the 18th and 19th centuries.

Although I have researched many books that were written in times long past, with references to various little white dogs, the earliest book I have found that does mention the breed as a Bichon Ténériffe, or a Bichon a Poil Frisé, was published not so very long ago, in 1959 in fact. It was written by Dr Fernand Mery of the Veterinary Academy of France. Dr Mery thought that the Bichon made its first appearance in the 15th Century. He considered the breed to be a cross between a Maltese and a small Barbet (spaniel) and a member of the Barbichon family. Dr Mery also postulated that the Bichon Ténériffe was none other than "Le Bichon à Poil Frisé classique". Does this mean a *classical* curly-coated lap dog?

THE ORIGINAL BICHON STANDARD

The original Standard for the Bichon Ténériffe was compiled by Madam Bouctovacniez, an authority on all Toy breeds, and was adopted by the FCI in 1933.

During 1934 Madam Bouctovacniez, in conjunction with the Friends of the Belgian Breeds, and Madam Nizet de Leemans, a breeder and international judge, subsequently suggested a more descriptive name for the breed than Bichon Ténériffe; hence the name Bichon Frisé, meaning a curly-coated

Entitled 'The Prince of Wales's Lap-dog', might it also be a Bichon?

This very early 19th century engraving of a Bichon illustrates how little the breed has altered.

lap-dog, was adopted. In the same year the Bichon Frisé was admitted to the French Stud Book and listed by the FCI as a French/Belgian breed.

As the breed had been admitted to the French Stud book and granted recognition by the Fédération Cynologique Internationale in 1934, Dr Mery could have been aware of Madam Nizet de Leemans' suggestion that the name should be changed from Bichon Ténérife to Bichon à Poil Frisé – that is, a curly coated lap dog

A 19th century engraving illustrates 'le Bichon', which is not unlike the Bichon of today. The German words seem to refer to the Bichon as 'a Polish Hound'! This engraving also depicts a Lowchen, Le Petit Chien Lion.

The Bichon Frisé as we know it today was originally called the Bichon Ténériffe or the Canary Islands Lapdog. Juba, King of Mauretania, who died in 46BC, made an expedition to the Canary Islands during his lifetime. An account of this expedition was preserved by Pliny the Elder. He mentions Canaria, so-called for the "multitude of dogs of great size" which were found there – which does not seem to bear much relation to our small Bichons.

One other item of interest from Dr Mery's book is the Bichon's relation of height to weight which he gives as: "Height 27 cms to 30 cms ($10^1/_2$-12 ins): Weight 2.5 kg to 4 kg ($5^1/_2$-9 lbs)". The breed today has the same height but the weight of our Bichons is somewhat heavier, between 5kg and 6kg.

THE BARBICHON GROUP

It is generally accepted that the Bichon Frisé is a member of the Barbichon group of dogs. This group is said to consist of the following breeds: the Maltese, the Bolognese, the Havanese (The Havana Silk Dog), The Coton du Tuléar, the Lowchen (Little Lion Dog) and the Bichon Frisé. I have also heard of the Bichon Manille, the Bichon Baléares and the Bichon de Pérou, but

The Havanese: Mrs Wilson's Tammylan Senza for Tollymore.

The Bolognese: Carol Alcock's Tammylan Coquotte with Bochin.

The Lowchen: Jocelyn Creefield's Ch. Melfield Goodness Gracious. Top Lowchen 1996 and 1997, winner of 23 CCs.   Russell Fine Art.

these last three breeds seem to have completely disappeared.

According to legend, Spanish sailors were responsible for the distribution of these little dogs. Four of the six breeds are said to have originated in the Mediterranean area, where voyages between ports were relatively short.

The Coton de Tuléar is indigenous to the Malagasy Republic (formerly Madagascar) and the port of Tuléar, off the south-east coast of Africa, in the Indian Ocean. The Havanese is said to be indigenous to Cuba in the Caribbean. In the age of sail, if the Coton de Tuléar and the Havanese had originated from the Mediterranean, they would have had to endure two very long sea voyages indeed

The Maltese, the Bolognese, the Coton de Tuléar and the Bichon, have quite a lot in common, with their dark eyes, dark pigment and white coats. The Lowchen and the Havanese come in a variety of coat colours but they also have a structural resemblance and a similar facial expression to their white-coated cousins.

In these first four breeds from the Barbichon group it is the coat texture which shows the greatest variation. The Maltese has a long straight coat of silky texture without an undercoat, the Bolognese coat is long and flocked, without any curl, the Lowchen's coat is long and wavy without curl, and all colours are acceptable. The Havanese coat is flat and soft, rarely white, more often light or dark beige, Havana grey or white, marked by these colours. The Coton de Tuléar coat is slightly coarse, with a texture of cotton, without an undercoat, whereas the Bichon's coat is always white and falls into soft and silky corkscrew curls with an undercoat

The Maltese: Vicky Herriff's beautiful Ch. Snowgoose The King's Ransom. Winner of 18 CCs, 18 Best of Breed, two Best in Show, and eight Groups.

which gives the coat, when first bathed and scissored, both the feel and look of a powder puff.

THE MALTESE

There have been many books written on the Maltese with a well-authenticated history which has been traced back many centuries. Strabo, circa AD 25, wrote that "there is a town in Sicily called Melita, whence are exported many beautiful dogs called Canes Melitaei. They were peculiar favourites of the women; but now there is less account made of these animals, which are not bigger than common ferrets or weasels, yet they are not small in understanding nor unstable in their love."

Dr Johannes Caius (1510-1573) in 1570 wrote a treatise entitled *Of Englishe Dogges* and mentioned the Maltese, referring to it as "a tiny breed of dog". Dr Caius claimed that "They are called Meliti, of the Isle of Malta, whence they were brought hither." 300 years later Idestone, in his book *The Dog* (1872), referring to the Maltese, commented that "a woolly coat is also found but the silky glistening hair is the only coat allowed." Is it possible that the woolly-coated Maltese was the original Bichon Frisé? Idestone's description of the weight, length and type of coat, with black eyes and nose, short but not chubby face, tallies very much with the Maltese we see today. The Maltese has a well-documented history that goes back, it is claimed, to 8,000 BC, but when relating the past history of the Bichon Frisé very little can be verified.

LITTLE WHITE DOGS IN ART

Over the centuries small white dogs have been depicted in several works of art. There are many paintings by Goya which include small white dogs. These dogs have, for many years, been referred to by hopeful and wishful-thinking breeders as Toy Poodles, Maltese, Lowchens (Little Lion Dog, due to the lion clip) and, more recently, the Bichon

The Duchess of Alba, Goya, 1795. Madrid, Prado Museum.

Frisé and the Bolognese. As there were no such thing as records or pedigrees in those far-off days there is no way of knowing with certainty their true breeding. The Bichon Tenerife, as the breed was then called, became very popular as the pampered pets to the ladies in the French Courts of Francis I (1515-1547). The breed's popularity with the aristocracy continued during the reign of Henri III (1574-1589).

Francis José Goya (1746-1828) became Court painter in the Spanish Courts of Charles IV in 1789, retaining this position during the French occupation of Spain under Joseph Bonaparte. Goya's paintings of the nobility often portray a small, white, curly-coated dog, often in the lion clip. This clip shows that the coat on the back, from the ribs to the hocks, had been completely removed.

During the 18th century a little white curly-coated lapdog resembling our Bichon became popular with the English aristocracy. It is said that these little pets helped to keep the ladies warm in their large, albeit sparsely heated, stately homes and castles.

An English artist prominent during the reigns of George II and George III, Sir Joshua Reynolds (1723-1792), first President to the Royal Academy, also included a curly-coated white lapdog in his portraits of ladies in Society. One example, *Miss Nellie O'Brien*, can be viewed at the Wallace Collection in London. Another, *The Ladies Annabel*

16

Miss Nellie O'Brien, Sir Joshua Reynolds, c. 1760.
The Wallace Collection.

Buy A Dog Ma'am, Richard Andsell, 1860.
Kennel Club, London.

Georgina, Countess of Spencer with her
daughter. Sir Joshua Reynolds, 1760-61.
The Earl of Spencer, Althorp.

Cat and Kittens.

Bichon with Bow.

and Mary Jemima Yorke, can be seen in the Cleveland Museum of Art, USA.

Sometime during the later part of the 19th century the Bichon's popularity as a highly-prized and pampered pet in the royal courts of France, Spain and England declined, but with its charming character and ability to learn and perform tricks, it was employed in many a circus and fair and, so it is said, eventually left to roam the streets, which I find difficult to believe.

RESCUING THE BICHON
The French soldiers of the First World War, on returning home, brought with them these little white dogs which they had found wandering in the ruins of the towns and villages of a Europe ravaged by the war. We owe a debt of gratitude to the French and Belgian devotees of the dog for recognising the value of these little Bichons rescued by the soldiers, as these breeders instigated a breeding programme which culminated in the recognition of the breed by the FCI some time after 1918.

However, the history of the Bichon Frisé is still fairly sparse. That it originates from the Mediterranean seems certain, and also that it was for many years known as the Bichon Tenerife.

As the dogs portrayed in the many paintings of the 17th and 18th Century certainly look like Bichons, we can only wonder what they were called before they came to be known as the Bichon Tenerife so many years later. These dogs have, at one time, been cosseted by royalty, and at another time been objects of barter by sailors. It is a difficult transition to understand.

I learnt from the late Mrs Jenkins who was for many years President of the Poodle Club, that she clearly remembered, during her many voyages

Meissen model of a Bolognese.

to West Africa in the 1920s, travelling on the P & O Liners when they called at the Canaries. The local inhabitants, rowing their small boats alongside the liners, offered for sale to the passengers little curly-coated white dogs, which Mrs Jenkins was convinced were identical to the Bichon Frisé which arrived in England in 1974.

The Meissen factory early in the 18th century produced many porcelain dog models referred to as the Bolognese, a breed which became very popular in the courts of Louis XV, but, as far as I am aware, models of the Bichon Frisé were never produced by the Meissen Factory.

THE MILTON LINES

When tracing the ancestry of the Bichons of today the names of M. and Mme Bellotte's Milton Kennels of Belgium are the most prolific; the Milton affix can be found in the oldest of pedigrees.

It appears that M. Bellotte bought his first male Bichon, Pitou, who was born in March 1924, sired by an unregistered dog called Tom out of an unregistered bitch named Mirette. Although the parentage of both Tom and Mirette was unknown, Pitou was registered with a first-class pedigree by the Société Royale Saint Hubert's *Livre des Origines*. Pitou, when mated to an unregistered bitch of unknown parentage named Diane, produced a bitch, Dony, born circa 1928. Dony became the first Bichon bitch to be registered with a

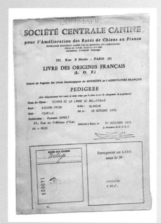

An Early French pedigree with Fr. Bel. & Int. Ch. Bandit de Steren Vor in the background.

An early Belgian pedigree with Pitou, born 1924, in the fourth generation.

first-class pedigree. The first Bichon to be bred with the Milton affix, a bitch named Dora of Milton, born in 1929, sired by Pitou out of his daughter Dony, was the start of 32 years of intensive in-breeding. Pitou, mated to Dora of Milton produced, in 1931, the first Belgian Champion, Bel. Ch. Pitou of Milton.

As I have discovered in my research, the Milton affix is to be found in the background of most Bichon bloodlines. When studying the early three-and four-

An early German Bichon, Iwan Von Dandelion. Note the natural, curly coat.

generation French pedigrees, the Milton Bichons were the only ones with a registered number, although several of the unregistered dogs were imported from Tenerife.

The earliest Steren Vor pedigree I have seen of French Bichons bred by Madame Adabie is of a bitch, Aress de Steren Vor, born in 1951. This is a third-class pedigree but Joy of Milton is in the third generation. In studying the pedigree of a famous Bichon, Fr. Bel. Int. Ch. Bandit de Steren Vor, 1952, the Milton prefix occurs no less than three times in the fourth generation.

THE AMERICAN INFLUENCE

The worldwide popularity of the Bichon Frisé is no doubt due to the breed's arrival in the USA in 1958, although it was not officially recognised by the American Kennel Club until 1973. American Bichon breeders devised a method of presentation which improved the breed out of all recognition; by grooming and scissoring the dog to show off the beauty of its coat, the Bichon became not only a popular pet dog but a very

BEL. CH. PITOU OF MILTON

Born 1931.
Breeder/Owner Mons. A. Bellotte

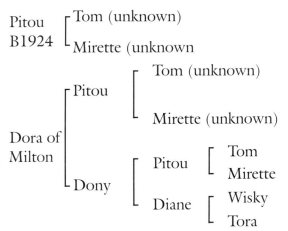

successful show dog, handled in the ring by many of America's top professional handlers, winning many Bests in Show and Non-sporting Groups.

When I first judged the breed in its natural state on the Continent in 1977 I understood why the Bichon in the past had never gained the popularity that it enjoys today – and it is thanks to the Americans.

FR. BEL. INT. CH. BANDIT DE STEREN VOR

Born June 1952.
Breeder/Owner Madame M. Abadie

			Joy of Milton
		FR CH Lucky De Mortessard	
			Gitane De Mortessard
	Uistiti		
			Sagille
		Teddy	
			Sami
Amy De Merleroux			
			FR. CH. Lucky De Mortessard
		Uistiti	
			Teddy
	Xette de Thérouenne		
			Agille
		S' Poucette	
			Alarme

FR. BEL. INT. CH. BANDIT DE STEREN VOR

			Joy Of Milton
		FR. CH. Lucky De Mortessard	
			Gitane De Mortessard
	Uistiti		
			Sagille
		Teddy	
			Sami
Aress De Steren Vor			
			Krysou
		Willy	
			Rirette
	Aress De Steren Vor		
			Willy
		Xa	
			Uouette

21

2 SELECTING YOUR BICHON PUPPY

Before you finally decide to buy a Bichon puppy do take into consideration how much of your time will be needed when the puppy joins the family. A young puppy in its early days requires as much, if not more, care and patience than a very young child. Put a baby in its cot or playpen and you know it is safe. Not so with a playful puppy.

THE BICHON'S BASIC NEEDS

The Bichon Frisé is a lapdog. It needs human company most of the time, so do not contemplate owning a Bichon if the house is left empty for long periods. Whether you intend buying a Bichon as a pet or as a potential show dog, several things should be considered carefully before you introduce a puppy into your home.

Young puppies in their first days

Time and patience is required when taking on a Bichon puppy.

Photo: Marc Henrie.

require a lot of care and patience and will need much of your time; this time spent in early training will be amply rewarded.

The Bichon has many advantages. Its small size makes it suitable for the family with a small house and garden, or city apartment, although it is equally at home in the country. However, although it is by tradition a lapdog, exercise is still essential.

A Bichon does not shed its coat, so you will not find hairs all over the furniture, but the beautiful white curly coat which, no doubt, was one of the features that attracted you to the breed, must be groomed daily. Unless you are able to bathe, brush and scissor the coat yourself, your dog will require regular visits to a grooming parlour, which is an added expense. The Bichon coat, if neglected, will turn into a solid mat, and that conditon can only be remedied by the complete removal by clippers of all the matted coat.

WHICH SEX?

When deciding which sex there are pros and cons. Both dogs and bitches are, in my opinion, equal in companionship and intelligence. Bitches come into season twice a year, immediately becoming a great attraction to all males in the vicinity, which can prove a little difficult if you are living in a built-up area; dogs are a little more difficult to house-train. Bitches can be spayed and dogs castrated if you so wish.

Lena Martindale with her 'Bylena' puppies. The responsible breeder will be only too happy to offer help and advice.

WHERE TO BUY

When buying a puppy of any breed always buy from a reputable breeder. A visit to any dog shows where Bichons are exhibited is a good idea, as there you will meet breeders who, after they have shown their dogs, will be only to pleased to advise you about where you can purchase a well-bred puppy of quality.

In any case always buy from a breeder where you will be able to see the puppies with their mother, which will enable you to judge how the puppies have been raised. Also, seeing the puppies' mother will give you some idea how the puppies will look as adults.

Any reputable breeder will be only too pleased to answer any questions and will show you the litter with pride. The breeder will probably ask several questions about your suitability to own one of the puppies. Do not be surprised at these questions; it shows that the breeder really cares about the puppies' future welfare.

CHOOSING YOUR BICHON

Having decided on a breeder, when you visit the kennels to see the litter and select your puppy, bear in mind the following points.

Make sure the eyes are clear and free from discharge; the eyes should be dark with black eye rims. Check the mouth: the gums should be pink and healthy,

the teeth pure white. The inside of the ears should be pink without any sign of a brown discharge. Run your fingers through the coat and make sure it is spotlessly clean. If selecting a male puppy, check that the two testicles are in evidence.

If you think that you might want to show your puppy then look at a few other points more closely. The puppy's shape should be square, the same from withers to ground as from withers to tail-set. If the puppy appears long in back or short on leg, the chances are that these faults will remain the same when the dog is fully grown. The colour, size and shape of the eyes are important. Pigmentation on the nose and pads should be black and unbroken; this is especially important on the nose. Check the bite: the teeth should be even, with a scissor bite. Watch how the puppy moves. The coat should be

Puppies with solid pigmentation are often born with apricot markings which fade quite quickly.

Bichon puppies are hard to resist – but try to keep a cool head when making your choice.

white, dense and curly; beware the sparse coat. The puppy's temperament must be outgoing and friendly, and the tail carried over the back with only the hair touching the back.

THE PROMISING SHOW PUPPY

When we consider how attractive all puppies, and especially the Bichon Frisé, are at eight weeks of age, it is impossible for even the most experienced breeder to be absolutely sure that any particular puppy will be of 'show' quality until he reaches six months. He can be a 'promising' puppy, but that is all any breeder can predict with a degree of certainty before that age.

As the puppy grows, even the most attractive puppy of eight weeks can alter beyond recognition. There are so many facets that may, and often do, go wrong. A pet puppy, as long as he or she is fit and healthy, does not require the near-

perfection needed by the show dog.

The head can coarsen, the muzzle can grow too long, the eyes, which must be dark, may lighten, the puppy can grow too long in back or become too leggy, the coat can become coarse, sparse or too straight. Pigment can fade, and the movement can be seen to be unsound.

The Bichon can have a perfect bite at eight weeks but when he cuts his second teeth the bite may become undershot or overshot, which is unacceptable in a show specimen. Eight-week-old puppies may grow too big or for that matter remain too small. All these undesirable points would be a drawback in the show ring for the mature Bichon Frisé.

However, if you are really serious about showing, it is possible to buy from an experienced breeder a promising puppy, a puppy that looks like a potential show specimen. It really is a matter of luck: many a promising

Ann Lee's budding 'Warmingham' puppies.
It takes an expert eye to assess show potential.

puppy has become just a 'pet' and many a 'pet' puppy has turned out to be of show quality. If you wish to buy a top-quality Bichon Frisé, wait until you can buy one at six months or older, as only at that age can you and the breeder be sure that it is of 'Show Quality'.

Here are a few hints which could be of assistance when looking for a promising 'show' puppy.

As I have said, always ask the breeder to let you see the mother of the litter from which you are making your selection; any obvious faults in her may very easily come out in one or two of her puppies as they mature. Make sure that all the litter are of a friendly and outgoing nature, a shy puppy should be avoided, as show dogs need to be very outgoing.

Ask the breeder to divide the sexes and for a short while just study the puppies of the sex you require, taking note of their general behaviour and movement. Usually one puppy will seem rather bossy, and that is the one, all other points being equal, to choose.

For a closer examination, stand the puppy on a firm table, always keeping a hand on him – puppies have a habit of jumping very quickly and they have no idea of height or distance. The muzzle should be short at this age, the skull behind the eyes should be broad. The ears should be set just above eye-level, with the leathers, which are thin, reaching halfway down the muzzle, with the inner ear pink and clean.

Look for dark, round, fairly large eyes, forward-looking without showing any white and well-spaced with a keen, intelligent expression. A scissor bite is essential and the teeth should be white and even, with tight black lips. The

body should feel firm; even at eight weeks the length of neck and the lay-back of shoulder can be assessed.

The back should be level with a high-set tail which is carried curved over the back but not touching; always make sure the tail is quite straight without any kink or bend.

The front legs should be quite straight when viewed from the front. The back legs should have a good bend of stifle. Feet must turn neither in nor out, and be tight and round with well-cushioned pads.

The pigment on the nose, lips, eye-rims and pads must be unbroken black. The skin over the inner corner of the eyes should also be well pigmented; this area of dark skin is referred to as the "haloes". Without these haloes the true Bichon Frisé expression is quite lost.

The puppy coat is rather difficult to judge, but a thin, sparse coat or a coat of a coarse texture should be avoided. Look for a thick, soft, dense, fairly long curly coat.

Quite often puppies are born with apricot or beige markings on the ears and parts of the body. Providing this is fairly pale the colour will usually fade as the puppy matures.

The puppy's temperament must be outgoing and friendly. As I have mentioned before, a subdued or shy puppy is quite useless in the show ring, and if you are selecting a male make certain that he is entire, with two apparently normal testicles descended into the scrotum.

PAPERWORK
Finally, having chosen your puppy, you should receive from the breeder several important details: a diet sheet, meal

times, the dates when the puppy was treated for worms, the pedigree and, last but by no means least, your national Kennel Club registration form which will enable you to transfer the puppy into your own name.

Breeders are usually proud of their puppies and will be only too pleased if, on purchase, the puppy is taken immediately to your vet for a certificate of general health; at the same time arrangements can be made for the puppy's first inoculations. An inoculation against parvovirus is usually given at eight weeks but the main course of inoculations commences at twelve weeks.

Until the puppy has received all its inoculations, do not let it associate with other dogs or walk in public places. At this age puppies are prone to infection.

The diet sheet given by the breeder should, as far as possible, be followed, as a change of diet at this early age can often upset a puppy's digestion, making him feel quite ill.

PREPARATIONS

There are several things you will need in preparation for the puppy's arrival in your home. He or she will need a bed and bedding, a feeding bowl, a water bowl, a comb and brush, and a soft collar and lead.

As young puppies chew everything while teething, there is little use in buying a basket or bed until he is older. A better idea is a strong cardboard box with one end cut down, which can be renewed as necessary. Make sure that the box is not bound together with staples which could harm the puppy. Line the box with a fluffy blanket and put the box in a quiet, warm corner out of the family's way

I strongly recommend using a playpen made especially for dogs which is similar to those made for children. A playpen big enough to take the dog's bed and a small area for newspaper is worth its weight in gold, and the dog will soon it accept as its own. On the occasions when it is necessary for the puppy to be left on his own in the house, and also during the night, you

Bichons love children – but make sure they are closely supervised.

Photo: Marc Henrie.

can rest assured that he will come to no harm when left safe and secure in a pen. These puppy pens can be purchased from most good pet shops and they come in sections so they can be easily dismantled.

THE HOMECOMING

Everything will be both strange and frightening to a puppy when he first arrives in your home. He has never been alone, he will have slept and played with his brothers and sisters and be quite unused to being on his own. The first days can be difficult but he will eventually settle down.

He must, however, very quickly learn to recognise his name and to obey you when you use it. Always use a very stern voice when he does wrong and a kind gentle voice when giving praise. A puppy will fall if he is left on a chair or table as he is used to being on the ground level and has no knowledge of heights, so always keep a firm hand on him.

Young children should only be allowed to hold a very young puppy while sitting on the floor, as puppies have a great habit of giving a sudden leap unless held very firmly. Be careful when opening or shutting doors when the puppy is loose. All electric plugs and wires must be kept out of the puppy's way.

THE FIRST NIGHT

Without a doubt the first night always presents problems which are difficult to solve. The puppy, finding himself alone, will be frightened and probably cold, and unless you are very lucky, will voice that misery by howling constantly. This you must either ignore, in the hope that the puppy will tire himself out, or else you can take the puppy up to bed in your room; but unless you are prepared for the puppy to sleep in your room from then on, this is very unsatisfactory. A warm stone hot-water bottle wrapped in a blanket, and a well-protected ticking clock placed in the puppy's bed can help, but in any case, after a few nights, the puppy will learn to settle down quietly. If he makes a noise, do not go in to the room to see him, just knock on the door and tell him to be quiet.

3 CARING FOR YOUR BICHON FRISE

There are several important things worth remembering in caring for your Bichon. Do keep all dog dishes absolutely clean. If the food is not eaten within ten minutes, do not be tempted to leave it down for the puppy to eat later. There are two reasons for not leaving food down: firstly a dog should be encouraged to eat his food quickly, and this he will learn to do if, after a short time, the food is removed. Secondly, any food left down will attract flies which can contaminate the food, often causing gastro-enteritis at the worst or an upset stomach at the very least, both of which can be easily avoided with a little care.

Puppies up to the age of approximately six months require four meals a day. Always feed at the same time each day, so organise these meals to fit in with the family timetable. It really does not matter which times you choose providing they are always the same, and properly spaced out. The number of meals can be gradually reduced as the puppy matures.

BREAKFAST: a little cereal or rusk (puppy kibble) moistened with warm water or broth. Twice a week a little scrambled egg with toast will be appreciated.

MID-DAY: a small portion, three to four ounces, of cooked beef, chicken, or fish, either minced or cut in small pieces, with all bones removed, mixed with biscuit or brown bread (puppy kibble).

LATE AFTERNOON: same as breakfast.

DINNER: similar to lunch.

A biscuit at bedtime is appreciated.

Fresh water must always be available. Do not leave the bowl in the sun. Never

A well-balanced diet is vital while puppies are growing.   Photo: Marc Henrie.

give cooked bones – a cooked bone will splinter; a raw beef bone is good for puppies' teeth, and raw bones do not splinter. It is wise to stick to the same diet both for puppies and for adults. As I have said, a sudden change in diet usually causes a stomach upset.

There are some very good commercial complete puppy and adult foods available. Any of these, fed according to the label, will be found to be satisfactory. After a meal the puppy must always be allowed to rest for at least 15 minutes.

EYE STAINS
Bichons are inclined to stain badly under the eyes unless they are wiped constantly, especially after the puppy has been asleep. Just use a small piece of damp cottonwool (cotton) to remove any discharge – prevention is better than cure. There is an ointment available especially for this staining under the eyes. Your vet or your puppy's breeder should be able to help you to obtain this.

GROOMING
The eight-week-old puppy docs not require much grooming. Nevertheless it is a good idea to get the puppy used to the brush and comb from the very first, before the coat matures and requires constant attention. Place a towel on a firm table and get the puppy to lie on his side. Gently hold him down with one hand, and give praise when he lies still, which he will soon learn to do while you groom the coat. Never take both hands off the puppy when he is on the table. Puppies move very quickly when unrestricted, and a fall from any height, however small, may cause an injury.

Section the hair, resting one hand on the roots. Starting at the coat ends, brush and comb upwards, and repeat all over the coat, not forgetting the arms and legs or the undersides. Turn the puppy over and repeat until the whole coat is free of tangles.

You will need only a brush, comb and nail clippers when the puppy is young. For the older dog you will need two

The Bichon puppy should get used to grooming and handling from an early age.

pairs of scissors, one with blunt tips necessary for cutting the hair around the eyes, and one pair for cutting any untidy hairs.

BATHING

Use a large basin or the family bath, with a rubber mat so the dog does not slip. Test the water; it should be fairly warm but not too hot. Place a small piece of cotton wool in each ear to prevent water entering the inside of the ear. Make sure there are no tangles or mats in the coat; in particular check under the arms and legs; these areas mat very easily. Bathing a puppy without checking that it is free of tangles or mats will result in a matted area which is impossible to remove without the use of scissors.

Wet the puppy thoroughly using a mixer spray, then shampoo all over, taking care not to allow any soap to get in the eyes; a baby shampoo is useful when washing the face. Rinse very thoroughly, then apply a conditioner and rinse again. The final rinse must be very thorough as soap or conditioner left in the coat can cause skin irritation, and it also leaves the coat looking dry and lifeless.

Wrap the puppy in a warm towel and towel-dry, then with a hair dryer set at a medium heat, blow-dry the coat, at the same time brushing the hair with a soft pin or bristle brush, drying a small area at a time. Once the puppy is completely dry, run the comb through the complete coat.

NAILS

Nails must not be allowed to get too long, especially the dewclaws as these will grow back into the skin if they are neglected. Light-coloured nails are easy to cut as the vein can be seen; the black nails often found on the Bichon are more difficult. Hold the foot firmly, clipping a little at a time. If a nail bleeds, a touch of potassium permanganate (or any coagulant) will stop the bleeding quickly. White dogs seem to be extra sensitive when their nails are cut; if your puppy objects too much, a visit to the vet will be necessary.

TEETH

The teeth must always be kept free of tartar. Do not let the tartar accumulate as it is easy to remove with the right tool which can be purchased from pet shops. A toothpaste made especially for dogs is now available.

EARS

The ears should be clean and sweet smelling. Any sign of a brown discharge needs veterinary attention immediately, as ear infections, if ignored, become very difficult to eradicate. Just sprinkle a little proprietary ear (baby) powder in the ear and gently pluck out any hair that is growing down the ear canal using your fingers.

TRIMMING

Puppies need very little trimming. Just scissor any hair that falls over the eyes. Cut any wispy hair on the body, making the coat an even length all over. Cut hair short under the tail and around the bottom of the feet. Do not cut the ears, moustache, beard or tail; these areas should be left to grow long and abundant.

THE TEENAGER

There will come a time in the puppy's life, usually at about four to five months, when you will wonder why you have kept him. This is called the ugly stage. The puppy looks unbalanced, gangly and lacking in coordination. The mouth, in the teething stage, can appear disastrous.

Most puppies go through this phase and many an owner who had dreams about showing the puppy has, at this stage, sold their Bichon on as a pet – only to regret it bitterly later, on

As your puppy gets a little older, you will find he has plenty of energy.

Photo: Marc Henrie.

33

discovering that the ugly duckling has turned into a swan. So do be patient because, before too long, your puppy will return to being the beauty he was before, whether or not he or she is destined for the show ring. Your pet Bichon will be the most beautiful pet.

THE MATURE BICHON

Most small breeds reach maturity by the time they are a year old and the Bichon is no exception. At this age they should no longer treated as puppies. By 12 months they will be fully grown, their second teeth will have completely erupted and they will only require one meal a day. The coat is more or less mature by 12 months although, in the Bichon, the really dense and fully grown coat is, in my opinion, at its best when the Bichon is nearly two years of age. By that time the feathering on the face, ears and tail will have grown long and abundant.

FEEDING

Once the Bichon reaches the age of twelve months one meal a day is sufficient. This meal can be given at any time that suits the family but must always be given at the same time each day. Never leave the food down if it has not been eaten within 10 minutes. All dogs should eat their food as soon as it has been prepared. If the food is left around they will become finicky eaters, which is always a nuisance. Please do try not to give your Bichon too many

Ch. Jacqueline Of Leijazulip At Tresilva – a beautiful portrait of a mature Bichon.
Photo: Marc Henrie.

treats. As a breed they are inclined to put on too much weight with great ease. Although protein is considered essential for the canine race, some Bichons appear to fare better on a diet low in protein.

The quantities of food that each dog requires will vary according to the amount of exercise and energy the dog

The author's Tresilva Virgil: Sire of four English Champions, two Norwegian, one German and one Italian Champion.

Photo: Marc Henrie.

expends during the day. Obviously if the dog leads a fairly sedate life style he will get far too fat if given as much food as the dog that is constantly rushing around and given long walks. A rough guide is considered to be 20 gms of food per 500 gms (^{3}/4 oz per 1 lb) body weight.

COAT CARE
As you now know, the Bichon does not shed its coat. This is a great advantage – no hairs on the furniture or on your clothes – but there is a price to pay for this boon. Daily grooming is essential, especially during the autumn and spring when the dog is changing its coat. The discarded hair stays in the thick coats and must be removed before it turns into a dense mat. If neglected the coat will turn into a solid tangle which can only be removed by stripping off the entire coat, resulting in a hairless wonder with little resemblance to the attractive curly-coated dog you have always admired. And, what is more, the

*The mature
Bichon head.*

coat takes a very long time to grow back.

Never bath a Bichon if the coat is matted. It is impossible to comb out mats once they are wet, as they become solid lumps, only removable in one piece with scissors.

A daily grooming is far the most satisfactory way of preventing the formation of mats. With a slicker brush start at the end of the coat working upwards towards the skin, removing tangles with care. Keep one hand on the roots to prevent any discomfort to the dog, then comb right down to the skin. Take particular notice of the areas behind the ears and under the arms and legs.

To look its best the Bichon should not be allowed to get too dirty. Prevent eye staining by gently wiping under the eyes in the morning and remember to wipe the beard with a damp cloth after eating. For hygienic reasons wipe the male dog's sheath regularly.

EXERCISE

Although the Bichon Frisé is a small dog it is remarkably sturdy and will enjoy as much exercise as many of the larger breeds. Bichons who live in the country have been known to follow horses and even to catch the occasional rabbit. A quick walk is really quite inadequate. The Bichon needs room to run, jump and play, thereby exercising all its muscles. You have only to watch a Bichon Frisé rushing around the garden to know that this is the exercise the Bichon prefers.

The amount of exercise can be safely left to the dog itself, as most dogs and puppies when running free will rest of their own accord once they get tired.

As the Bichon is so easy to train, the breed does well in both the Agility and the Obedience classes.

THE OLD DOG

Bichons of course will vary, but if in good health, and with care, this breed often lives to quite a good age; between 11 and 13 years is a good average, although many have lived several years longer. But there will come a time when it is obvious that life has lost its meaning. The Bichon Frisé, with its white coat, does not show its age as quickly as dogs with black or dark coats whose muzzles will often turn grey as they get older. The only signs we see in the Bichon Frisé is a lack of activity and a slowing of movement, and their eyesight may deteriorate or they may suffers from a loss of hearing. Also the coat often becomes thin and sparse. It is even more important, as the dog ages, that the teeth are kept clean and free of tartar, as tartar can cause the gums to become badly infected and cause discomfort to the dog. Do consult your vet if this occurs, especially if the dog's breath has become unpleasant.

None of these signs of old age seem to bother the Bichon unduly, but do make sure that the dog is given extra comfort. An old dog must always be kept warm and out of draughts. Good nutritious food must be given regularly; older dogs will appreciate two meals a day.

There comes a time which we all dread, when we realise our cherished companion is in constant pain, completely lacking in any quality of life, and it is time to make the decision to give our faithful pet and friend of many years a quick and painless release from suffering. This is our final act of compassion and kindness; although so very sad and difficult, it must be done.

Bichons enjoy exercise, but they also enjoy their home comforts.

4 THE BREED STANDARDS

A Breed Standard is a blueprint that attempts to describe the ideal specimen of each breed. It is written for the guidance of breeders when planning a breeding programme and for judges who, by their ability to interpret the Standard, are able to place the exhibits at a show in the order which in their opinion conforms most closely to the Standard.

Standards are often altered slightly but, usually, these alterations are for minor points which breeders consider necessary for the welfare and future viability of the breed.

As will be appreciated when reading the following three Standards, slight differences do occur but the most important features of the Bichon are emphasized in all.

The Breed Standards of countries other than the UK more often than not

Ch. Tresilva Bright Spark at Suanalu, bred by the author, owned by Joan Gadd-Davies.

Photo: Yvette S. Caunter.

name or list the faults which are penalized, or severe faults which may call for a dog's elimination from the show ring. The KC Standards do not mention specific faults; these are dealt with in the following statement which comes at the end of each British Standard: "FAULTS: Any departure from the foregoing points should be considered a fault and the seriousness with which the fault should be regarded should be in exact proportion to its degree."

As all Breed Standards in the UK are based on a breed's country of origin I have listed the FCI Standard first, as the Bichon Frisé is considered to be a Belgian/French Breed.

GENERAL APPEARANCE
FCI: 1997 Classification: Group 9

Companion and Toys.
Lively and playful little dog, with a lively gait, medium length of muzzle, long loose corkscrew-curled hair, very like the coat of a Mongolian goat. Head carriage is proud and high, the eyes dark lively and expressive.

UK: 1994 Classification: The Toy Group.
Well balanced dog of smart appearance, closely coated with handsome plume carried over the back. Natural white coat curling loosely. Head carriage proud and high.
USA: 1988 Classification: The Non-Sporting Group.
The Bichon Frisé is a small sturdy white powder puff of a dog whose

The head is carried proud and high.

Photo: Marc Henrie.

Correct type.

Incorrect type.

merry temperament is evidenced by his plumed tail carried jauntily over the back and his dark-eyed inquisitive expression. This is a breed that has no gross or incapacitating exaggerations and therefore there is no inherent reason for lack of balance or unsound movement. Any deviation from the ideal described in the Standard should be penalized to the extent of the deviation. Structural faults common to all breeds are as undesirable in the Bichon Frisé as in any other breed, even though such faults may not be specifically mentioned in the Standard.

The FCI requirement for "a lively gait" is the only reference to movement in the FCI Standard.

The USA clause is easy to understand. However, the words "powder puff" may cause concern, as the natural

Bichon coat, even when trimmed, still has a certain amount of curl. The only way to achieve a "powder puff" effect is by bathing, brushing and scissoring. Even so, this powder-puff look does not last very long. The curly appearance soon returns, providing the coat is of the correct soft and silky texture. Pet Bichons look very curly two days after bathing. The American presentation, which has resulted in the breed's popularity in the show rings of the world, does result in a powder-puff effect.

FCI Standard's description of the coat as being 'very like the coat of a Mongolian goat' leaves a lot to our imagination, as most of us have never seen a Mongolian Goat.

CHARACTERISTICS
FCI: No separate clause.

UK: Gay, happy, lively little dog.

Am. Ch. Sterling Rumor Has It. In the summer of 1998 'Rumor' broke a long-standing record and became the top-winning Bichon of all time in the USA. Owned (and shown) by Paul Flores and Meriko Tamaki.

Photo: Backstage.

USA: No separate clause.

Bichon Frisé have such an enchanting character, they are gay and happy with the most amusing habits. Surely the character of all breeds should be included in all Standards.

TEMPERAMENT
FCI: There is no separate reference except that mentioned in the first clause –"Lively and playful".

UK: Friendly and outgoing.
USA: Gentle-mannered, sensitive, playful and affectionate. A cheerful attitude is the hallmark of the breed and one should settle for nothing less.

In this clause I like the American interpretation of temperament. I suppose it means much the same as friendly and outgoing but "gentle-mannered" is so true of the Bichon Frisé. A dour, miserable, bad-tempered or aggressive dog bears no resemblance to the Bichon Frisé.

HEAD AND SKULL
FCI: Skull: Rather flat to the touch although the coat makes it appear round. The skull longer than the muzzle. The muzzle must not be thick nor heavy, without, however, being snipy; the cheeks are flat and not very muscular. The furrow between the superciliary arches slightly visible. Nose is rounded,

Correct body proportions. Good expression.

Correct head proportions.　　*Poor head – small eyes, long muzzle.*　　*Incorrect proportions.*

black, finely grained. Stop not very marked.

UK: Ratio of muzzle length to skull length 3:5 on a head of the correct width and length. Lines drawn between the outer corners of the eyes and nose will create a near equilateral triangle. Whole head in balance with body. Muzzle not thick, heavy or snipy. Cheeks flat, not very strongly muscled. Stop moderate but definite, hollow between eyebrows just visible. Skull slightly rounded, not coarse, with hair accentuating rounded appearance. Nose large, round, black soft and shiny.

USA: Skull slightly rounded allowing for a round and forward-looking eye. The stop is slightly accentuated. Muzzle: a properly

42

balanced head is three parts muzzle to five parts skull, measured from the nose to the stop and from the stop to the occiput. A line drawn between the outside corners of the eyes and to the nose will create a near equilateral triangle. There is a slight degree of chiseling under the eyes, but not so much as to result in a weak or snipy foreface. The lower jaw is strong. The nose is prominent and always black.

The FCI calls for a "rather flat" skull, which I suppose is much the same as "slightly rounded". I have always considered that the width of the zygomatic arch is responsible for the forward-looking eyes. This arch is flat in the Poodle with its fine head and almond eyes. A Bichon lacking in width of skull will have almond eyes or small, close-set eyes.

Both the American and British Standards call for the equilateral triangle which, when correct, gives the true Bichon expression.

The ratio of muzzle to skull length, 3 to 5, is made clear in the USA clause as it states this measure should be taken "from stop to occiput".

Glory Be of Bobander showing a typical, attractive Bichon expression. Owned by Chris Wyatt, bred by Mrs D. Adams.

Photo: John Daniels.

nor prominent as in the Griffon Bruxellois and the Peke; the socket must not bulge. The eyeball must not stand out too much.

EYES
FCI: Dark eyes as much as possible with dark eyelids, of a rather round shape and not almond-shaped; not placed obliquely; lively not too big, not showing any white. Neither large

UK: Dark, round with black eye rims, surrounded by dark haloes, consisting of well pigmented skin. Forward-looking, fairly large but not almond-shaped, neither obliquely set nor protruding. Showing no white

43

when looking forward. Alert, full of expression.

USA: Soft, dark-eyed, inquisitive, alert. Round black or dark brown and are set in the skull to look directly forward. An overly large or bulging eye is a fault as is an almond-shaped obliquely set eye. Haloes, the black or very dark brown skin surrounding the eyes, are necessary as they accentuate the eye and enhance expression. Broken pigment or total absence of pigment on the eye rims produce a blank and staring expression which is a definite fault. Eyes of any other colour than black or dark brown are a very serious fault and must be severely penalized.

Late in the 1970s at a meeting between the AKC and the KC a decision was made to streamline the Standards. The KC went ahead with this decision and all the KC Standards were pared down, but the AKC decided to leave things as they were. The above two clauses illustrate this point. I personally would like the more detailed description and the inclusion of faults, although the UK Standard states all that is needed in fewer words. An earlier version of the FCI Standard stated "not showing any white when looking forward".

These three words are still in the UK Standard but not in the others. I think they are quite important as most dogs glancing sideward show some white of their eyes.

EARS
FCI: Drooping, well furnished with fine curly long hairs, carried rather forward when dog is attentive, but in such a way that the front edge touches the skull and does not stand away obliquely; the length of the cartilage must not, like in the Poodle, extend to the nose, but stops half way of the length of the muzzle. They are anyway not as wide and are finer than the Poodle.

UK: Hanging close to head, well covered with flowing hair longer than leathers, set on slightly higher than eye level and rather forward on skull. Carried forward when dog alert, forward edge touching skull. Leather reaching approximately half-way along muzzle.

USA: Ears are drooping and are covered with long flowing hair. When extended towards the nose, the leathers reach approximately halfway the length of the muzzle. They are set on slightly higher than eye level and rather forward on the skull, so that when alert they serve to frame the face.

The FCI and the UK both carry the following: "When alert the front edge of the Bichon's ears are carried forward, touching the skull." This emphasises that the ears should not fly outwards – quite an important feature.

MOUTH

FCI: Bite normal, i.e. the incisors of the lower jaw are placed immediately against and behind the point of the teeth in the upper jaw. Lips are fine, rather lean, less however than in the Schipperke, falling only enough so as to cover the lower lip, but never heavy or pendulous. They are normally black up to the corner of the lips, the lower lip must not be heavy nor visible, nor slack and does not allow the mucous membranes to be seen when the mouth is closed.

UK: Jaws strong, with a perfect, regular and complete scissor bite, i.e. upper teeth closely overlapping lower teeth and set square to the jaws. Full dentition desirable. Lips fine, fairly tight and completely black.

USA: Bite is scissors. A bite which is undershot or overshot should be severely penalised. A crooked or out of line tooth is permissible; however, missing teeth are to be severely penalised. Lips are black, fine and never drooping.

The FCI gives a more detailed description of lips than it gives for the skull. The reference to the lips being black up to the corner of the lips gives me the impression that the corners can lack pigmentation. When I visited the breeders in Belgium it was impressed upon me that any break in the pigmentation of the lips should be avoided as it indicated weak pigmentation. The UK Standard says "completely black" which is considered important.

The statement in the American clause that a crooked or out of line tooth is permissible does prevent judges from penalising a good dog for this one minor fault.

NECK

FCI: Reach of neck is fairly long, carried high and proudly. Round and fine near the skull, broadening gradually to merge smoothly into the shoulders. Its length is approximately a third of the length of the body (proportion of 11cm to 33cm for a dog 27cm high), the points of the shoulder-blades against the withers taken as basis.

UK: Arched neck fairly long, about one-third the length of the body. Carried high and proudly. Round and slim near head, gradually broadening to fit smoothly into shoulders.

USA: The arched neck is long and carried proudly behind an erect head; it blends smoothly into the shoulders. The length of the neck

from occiput to withers is approximately 1/3rd the distance from forechest to buttocks.

The USA Standard makes the proportions quite clear by stating that the length of body is "from forechest to buttocks". In Britain the wording would be different and more likely to read "from the point of shoulder to the pin bones." "Length of the body" can be open to misinterpretation. The proportions given in the FCI clause work out that a Bichon who measures 11 ins from withers to tail-set and from withers to ground will have a body length of 13.5 ins and a length of neck 4.25 ins. A well-balanced Bichon must have a good reach of neck.

FOREQUARTERS

FCI: Seen from the front, forelegs really straight and perpendicular; fine bone. The shoulder is fairly slanted, not prominent, giving the appearance of being the same length as the upper arm, about 10cm; does not stand away from the body, and the elbow in particular does not turn out. Upper arm not standing away from the body. Elbow not turned out. Pastern short and straight seen from the front, very slightly oblique seen in profile.

UK: Shoulders oblique, not prominent, equal in length to upper arm. Upper arm fits close to body. Legs straight, perpendicular, when

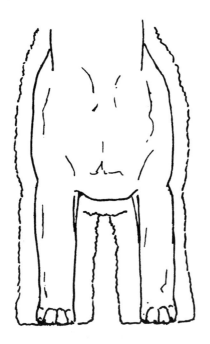

Correct front.

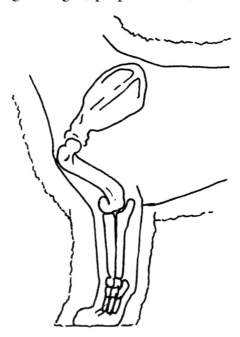

Correct shoulder angulation.

Ann Lee's Ch. Warmingham Scarlet O'Hara: Winner of 22 CCs, 9 BOBs.
Photo: John Hartley.

seen from front; not too finely boned. Pasterns short and straight viewed from front, very slightly oblique viewed from side.

USA: The shoulder blade, upper arm and forearm are approximately equal in length. The shoulders are laid back to somewhat near a forty-five degree angle. The upper arm extends well back so the elbow is placed directly below the withers when viewed from the side. Legs are of medium bone,

straight, with no bow or curve in the forearm or wrist. The elbows are held close to the body. The pasterns slope slightly from the vertical. The dewclaws may be removed.

Here we have three different interpretations regarding "bone". The FCI calls for fine bone, the USA medium bone and the UK not too finely boned. I think that the USA and UK mean more or less the same thing. I remember when we were compiling the first Interim Standard in 1975 we did not like "fine" (an Italian Greyhound has fine bone) and "medium" we considered similar to a Cocker, so we settled on "not too fine".

The lay-back of shoulder is given the ideal angle in the USA version; a dog with an upright shoulder does not have good frontal extension, and the stride will be limited in such an individual.

BODY
FCI: Loin broad and well muscled, slightly arched. Rump: slightly rounded. Chest: well developed, the sternum is pronounced, the false ribs rounded and do not end abruptly, the chest having horizontally a rather great depth.

UK: Forechest well developed, deep brisket. Ribs well sprung, floating ribs not terminating abruptly. Loin broad, well muscled, slightly arched and well tucked up. Pelvis broad,

Correct topline.

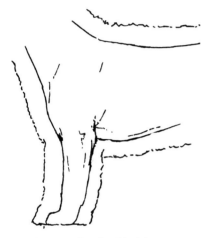

Correct depth of brisket.

Incorrect: Short upper arm, straight hindquarters.

croup slightly rounded. Length from withers to tail set should equal height from withers to ground.

USA: The chest is well developed and wide enough to allow free and unrestricted movement of the front legs. The lowest point of the chest extends at least to the elbow. The rib cage is moderately sprung and extends back to a short and muscular loin. The forechest is well pronounced and protrudes slightly forward of the point of shoulder. The underline has a moderate tuck-up.

Both the UK and FCI Standards refer to the false ribs which must not end abruptly. Once, in the distant past, I came across this fault; the false ribs are quite obvious as they are inclined to

Sue Dunger's Ch. Sulyka Puzzle, born 1987. Winner of 9 CCs, 5 BOBs. Photo: Thomas Fall.

stand out from the dog's sides. The slight rise over the loin must not be confused with a dog's topline that rides up at the back due to a short forearm.

The USA states the "forechest is well pronounced", the UK "well developed". The forechest is a part of the breast bone that slightly protrudes beyond the point of shoulder; the FCI states the "Sternum is pronounced." I believe the correct term for this slight protrusion is the "prosternum".

The UK Standard tells us that the length from withers to tail-set measures the same as from withers to ground. In my opinion this helps us to assess the correct balance between the height and length of the Bichon.

HINDQUARTERS

FCI: The pelvis is wide. Thighs: Broad and muscular; well slanting. Hocks: Compared with the Poodle, the hock joint is also more angulated.

UK: Thighs broad and well rounded. Stifles well bent; hocks well angulated and metatarsals perpendicular.

USA: The hindquarters are of medium bone, well angulated with muscular thighs and spaced moderately wide. The upper and lower thigh are nearly equal in length meeting at a well bent stifle joint.

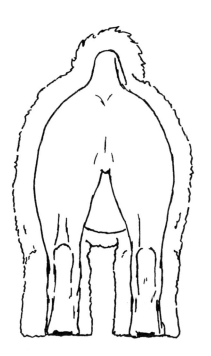

Correct parallel hocks.

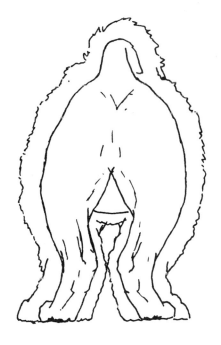

Incorrect – cow hocks.

As the description of "bone" was referred to under Forequarters and would be considered to apply to the whole skeleton of the dog, it was not thought necessary to repeat this clause in the UK Standard. "Spaced moderately wide" in the American clause is a worthwhile addition; so many Bichons move too close at the rear.

FEET

FCI: Sinewy. Nails preferably black; it is however an ideal difficult to obtain.

UK: Tight, rounded and well knuckled up. Pads black. Nails preferably black.

USA: Feet are tight and round, resembling those of a cat and point directly forward turning neither in or out. Pads are black. Nails kept short.

The FCI Standard does not convey anything to me at all. The lack of any mention of the pads I find surprising. Unless the pads are black, the dog's pigmentation will not be strong and lasting. Black nails are rare but to my knowledge the colour of the nails has little to do with strength of pigment, whereas weak and patchy colour of the pads does. The American comparison of the feet to those of a cat's paw is explicit, summed up in the UK by the words "Tight, rounded and well

knuckled up". The KC does not permit any reference to other animals in their Standards.

TAIL

FCI: The tail is set a little more below the back line than in the Poodle. Normally the tail is carried high and gracefully curved in line with the spine, without being rolled up; it is not docked and must not be in contact with the back; however, the tail furnishings may fall onto the back.

UK: Normally carried raised and curved gracefully over the back but not tightly curled. Never docked. Carried in line with backbone, only hair touching back; tail itself not in contact. Set on level with topline, neither too high nor too low. Corkscrew tail undesirable.

USA: Tail is well plumed, set on level with the topline and curved gracefully over the back so that the hair of the tail rests on the back. When the tail is extended towards the head it reaches at least halfway to the withers. A low set tail, a tail carried perpendicularly to the back, or a tail which droops behind is to be severely penalized. A corkscrew tail is a serious fault.

As the tail is required to be carried high in a curve, the set-on needs to be level with the topline; even when set-on just a fraction lower the curve over the back becomes too tight. The length of the tail also makes a difference; too short it becomes too tight, too long and it would touch the spine. Reaching halfway to the withers would be about right. If the set of the tail is correct it will be carried in a curve with only the hair touching the spine. A tail clamped on or touching the spine should be penalized.

In the FCI original Standard of 1933 the clause for Tail comes under the heading 'Le Rein': included are the words "pas tourné de côté" – not turning to the side!

GAIT AND MOVEMENT
FCI: Not mentioned separately.

UK: Balanced and effortless with an easy reach and drive maintaining a steady and level topline. Legs moving straight along line of travel, with hind pads showing.
USA: Gait: movement at a trot is free, precise and effortless. In profile the forelegs and hindlegs extend equally with an easy reach and drive that maintains a steady topline. When moving, the head and neck remain somewhat erect and as speed increases there is a very slight convergence of legs towards the center line. Moving away, the hindquarters travel with moderate width between them and the foot pads can be seen. Coming and going his movement is precise and true.

Two of these clauses agree in the main, although the American clause gives more detail. As so many Bichons move close behind, "hindquarters travelling away with moderate width" is a point to be noted. Only when moving with the correct drive will the black pads be seen.

COAT
FCI: Fine, silky, very loose corkscrew curls looking like the coat (fur) of the Mongolian goat, neither flat nor corded and 7cm to 10cm long. The dog may be shown with feet and muzzle slightly tidied up.

UK: Fine, silky, with soft corkscrew curls, neither flat nor corded, and measuring 7cm to 10cm in length. The dog may be presented untrimmed or have muzzle and feet slightly tidied up.
USA: The texture of the coat is of utmost importance. The undercoat is soft and dense, the outer coat of a coarser and curlier texture. The combination of the two gives a soft but substantial feel to the touch which is similar to plush or velvet and when patted springs back. When bathed and brushed, it stands off the body, creating an overall powder puff appearance. A wiry coat is not desirable. A limp, silky coat, a coat

Brenda Ellis' Honeylyn Sammy Soap Sud.

that lies down, or a lack of undercoat are very serious faults. Trimming: the coat is trimmed to reveal the natural outline of the body. It is rounded off from any direction and never cut so short as to create an overly-trimmed or squared-off appearance. The furnishings of the head, beard, moustache, ears and tail are left longer. The longer head hair is trimmed to create an overall rounded impression. The topline is trimmed to appear level. The coat is long enough to maintain the powder puff look which is characteristic of the breed.

In all countries governed by the FCI trimming of the breed is strictly forbidden. The Bichon is still presented at all FCI Shows in its natural coat. I have already commented on the words "powder puff". This American description does agree that this effect is achieved only after bathing and brushing. This section does mention the undercoat, which the British Standard omits. I am of the opinion that without the undercoat a Bichon lacks the correct soft and silky texture.

As Bichons in the UK are always exhibited in the American style of presentation, it is hoped that before too long this clause in the UK Standard on trimming will be amended. A coat 7-10 cms (3-4 ins), called for in the FCI clause, is for the untrimmed coat; nevertheless any coat less than 2 cms (1 in) is too short.

COLOUR

FCI: Pure white. The pigmentation beneath the white coat is preferably dark; the genitals are then pigmented either black, bluish or beige.

UK: White, but cream or apricot markings acceptable up to 18 months. Under white coat, dark pigment desirable. Black, blue or beige markings often found on skin.

USA: Color is white, may have shadings of buff cream or apricot around the ears or on the body. Any excess of 10 per cent of the entire coat of a mature specimen is a fault and should be penalized, but color of

Joan Gadd Davies' Tresilva Cupboard Love at Suanalu.

the accepted shading should not be faulted in puppies.

In Britain we do not accept any colour in the coat after 18 months of age. Although our puppies are often born with apricot marking these invariably fade with time, usually well before they are 18 months.

The testicles are usually black, the skin, although hidden under the dense coat, carries many dark areas of pigmentation.

SIZE

FCI: The height at the withers should not exceed 30cm, the small size being an element of success.

UK: Ideal height 23-28 cms (9-11 ins) at withers.
USA: Dogs and bitches 9.5 inches to 11.5 inches are to be given primary preference. Only where the comparative superiority of a specimen outside this range clearly justifies it should greater latitude be taken. In no case should this latitude extend over 12 inches or under 9 inches. The minimum limits do not apply to puppies.

The FCI Standard of 1972 is identical to the FCI Standard today. The Bichon is a Toy Breed and the French word 'Bichon' means lapdog. The clause 'the small size being an element of success' appeals to me.

FAULTS

Only the FCI gives a list of faults.
FCI: Slightly overshot or undershot mouth.

53

Pigmentation extending into the coat and forming rusty patches.
Coat flat, wavy or too short.

ELIMINATING FAULTS:
Pink nose. Flesh coloured lips. Light coloured eyes. Prognathism (under-shot over-shot) so developed to the extent that the incisors do not touch. Rolled up tail or twisted in a spiral. Black spots in the coat.
FCI: Note Male animals should have two apparently normal testicles fully descended into the scrotum.

UK: Male animals should have two apparently normal testicles fully descended into the scrotum.
UK: Any departure from the foregoing points should be considered a fault and the seriousness with which the fault should be regarded should be in exact proportion to its degree.

USA: Faults are included in each clause of the American Standard but there does not appear to be any reference regarding the testicles.

No two judges will interpret a Breed Standard in exactly the same way; providing their choice conforms to the Standard there is little cause for concern.

The words Bichon Frisé translated literally mean a curly coated lapdog, therefore one looks for a small dog not too heavy in weight, with a curly coat. The Bichon is considered to be a 'head' breed. Without the right proportions of skull to muzzle, the large, forward-looking dark and expressive eyes surrounded by haloes, and the black shiny nose, the dog will not have the typical Bichon expression. No matter how clever the presentation around the face, if the muzzle is too long or the eyes light, almond-shaped, close-set or small, or lacking haloes, the head will not have the typical Bichon expression and the dog will lack 'type'.

The Bichon, although small in size, has a firm and sturdy body, neither too long nor too short, straight forelegs, elbows close to the body and well angulated rear quarters. The tail must not touch the back, only the long tail feathering.

When moving, legs should be parallel with good reach and drive. There must be a level topline that does not slope up at the back. A good reach of neck is required – a third of the body length, which is stipulated, is a lot of neck. The coat must be soft and silky.

As it says in the USA Standard under General Appearance, the Bichon has no exaggerations, therefore one should look for balance and soundness. Balance is an harmonious blending of all the dog's features.

THE FIRST BREED STANDARD
I have in my possession four pages from a French magazine called *L'Éleveur, revue*

Cover of 'L'Eleveur'.

cynégétique et canine, which was founded in 1885 by Pierre Megnin, and the following information which was published in 1935. These four pages were issued on 13th October 1935, and are headed "Bichons, Maltais, Havanais et Cie" and it cosists of a most interesting and informative article referring to all the breeds in the Barbichon Group, except the Coton De Tulear, which I have mentioned in Chapter One on the history of the breed.

Breed Standards are issued for all breeds, but to be able to read an original Standard of any breed from its inception is a rarity. Edward Ash's

Practical Dog, published in 1930, does give a chapter on 'Description of British Breeds and their Show Points', but even these Standards are not original.

History tells us that breed clubs issued descriptions and a scale of points compiled by the most successful and experienced breeders. The Bulldog Club issued such a Standard in 1875, but to trace the original Standard of most breeds is difficult, to say the least.

As the Bichon Frisé was only recognised by the FCI in 1934, the following French Standard was the very first Breed Standard issued for our breed and therefore well worth preserving. Most clauses are more or less as we have in the present Standards, although it is surprising that this old Standard calls for the coat to be presented in 'Lion clip like a Poodle' but without the docked tail, and that the tail must not turn to one side.

BICHON de TÉNÉRIFFE
La FCI a baptisé ce chien de son appellation 'de Ténériffe' pour lui appliquer celui de 'bichon à poil frisé'. Voici le standard qu'elle a adopté pour lui.

STANDARD ADOPTÉ PAR LA FCI
Aspect général: Chiens à poil long, tout blanc et fin, d'aspect laineux, frisottant, ni plat, ni cordé atteignant de 7 à 12cm. Le port de la tête est fier et haut, les yeux foncés sont vifs et expressifs, de forme arrondie, pas en amande ni placés obliquement, mais pas

gros ni proéminents, oreille tombante, portée en avant, bien garni de poils frisés, mais pas très longue de cartilage. Sa hauteur au garrot ne doit guère dépasser 0m. 30, la petite taille étant un élément du succès.

Les proportions que nous citons en chiffres sont à rapporter à un chien de la taille de 0m. 27 au garrot.

Les membres sont fins et bien d'aplomb, l'allure est vive et gaie, le déplacement rapide et aisé, le caractère enjoué. Très affectueux envers le maître.

Il est généralement toiletté en lion, comme le caniche, mais la queue n'est pas encourtée; normalement, il la porte relevée et gracieusement recourbée, de façon que le panache retombe sur le dos mais sans être enroulée dans le plan de l'épine dorsale.

TÊTE: Le crâne, plus long que le museau, est dans la proportion de 8 à 5 centimètres, la circonference du crâne correspondant à la hauteur au garrot, soit 27 centimètres environ.

LA TRUFFE: est arrondie, bien noire, à grain fin et luisant.

LES LÈVRES: Seront fines, assez sèches, moins, toutefois, que chez le schipperke, légèrement tournées dans leur partie antérieure, ni tombantes que juste pourque la lèvre inférieure soit couverte, mais jamais lourdes ni pendantes; normalement pigmentées de noir jusqu'aux commissures; l'inférieure ne peut être lourde, ni apparente, ni molle, ne laissant pas voir les muqueuses dans l'attitude calme, c'est-à-dire quand la gueule est fermée.

LA DENTURE: est normale, c'est-à-dire que les dents incisives de la mâchoire inférieure viennent se juxtaposer immédiatement contre et derrière la pointe des dents de la mâchoire supérieure.

LE MUSEAU: ne doit pas être épais ni lourd, les joues plates mais cependant pas pincées, allongées, pas très musculeuses. Le stop est peu accentué, la gouttière entre les arcades sourcillères, légèrement apparente.

LES YEUX: foncés, autant que possible bordés de paupières noires, de forme plutôt arrondie et non en amande, ni placés obliquement, sont vifs, pas trop grands, ne laissant pas voir de blanc. Ils ne sont ni gros ni proéminents comme ceux du Griffon bruxellois et du pékinois, l'orbite ne doit pas être saillante. Le globe de l'oeil ne doit pas ressortir de façon exagérée.

LE CRÂNE: est plutôt plat au toucher, bien que la garniture la fasse paraître ronde.

LES OREILLES: Sont tombantes, bien garnies de poils finement frisés et longs, portées plutôt en avant à l'attention, mais de façon que le bord antérieur touche au crâne et ne s'en écarte pas obliquement; la longueur du cartilage ne doit pas aller, comme chez le caniche, jusqu'à la truffe, mais s'arrête à la moitié de la longueur du museau. Elles sont, du reste, bien moins larges et plus fines que chez ce chien.

L'ENCOLURE: Est assez longue, portée haut et fièrement. Elle est ronde et fine près du crâne, s'élargissant graduellement pour s'emboîter sans heurt dans les épaules.
Sa longueur est très approximativement un tiers de la longueur du corps [proportion de 11 à 33 centimètres] pour un sujet de 0m. 27 de haut, les pointes de l'épaule contre le garrot étant prises comme bases.

L'ÉPAULE: assez oblique, pas proéminente, de même longueur que le bras [10-10] celui-ci n'est pas écarté du corps et de la coude, particulièrement, n'est pas en dehors.

LES PATTES: sont droites vues de face, bien d'aplomb, fines d'ossature, le paturon court, droit, vu de face, très légèrement oblique, vu de profil. Les ongles seront de préférence noirs; c'est un idéal toutefois difficile à atteindre.

LA POITRINE: est bien développée, le sternum prononcé, les fausses côtes arrondies et ne finissant pas brusquement, la poitrine ayant horizontalement une assez grande profondeur.

LES FLANCS: Sont bien relevés au ventre, la peau y est fine et non flottante, de façon à donner une apparence assez levrettée.

LE REIN: est large et puissant, légèrement bombé. Le bassin est large, la croupe dodue, légèrement arrondie; le fouet, planté un peu plus sous la ligne du dos que chez le caniche, se relève gracieusement en courbe, mais bien dans le plan de l'épine dorsale [pas tourné de côté], la pointe et le panache retombant vers le milieu du dos. Les cuisses sont larges et bien musclées, les rayons bien obliques, le jarret est aussi plus court que chez le caniche, le pied nerveux.

PIGMENTATION: La pigmentation sous le poil blanc est foncée de préférence; les organes sexuels sont alors pigmentés de teinte noire ou bleuâtre, comme les taches et mouchetures que l'on rencontre souvent sur le corps.

LA TOILETTE: Se fait en lion, comme pour le caniche, sauf que la queue n'est pas écourtée.

DÉFAUTS GRAVES: Disqualifications: prognathisme inférieur [grignage]. Nez rose et lèvres couleur chair, yeux pâles, cryptorchidie, queue enroulée et tournée en hélice. Taches noires dans le poil. Défauts à éviter: pigmentation se prolongeant dans le poil de façon à former des taches rousses. Poil plat, ondulé, cordé ou trop court. Monorchidie.
Prognathisme supérieur. Chien trop enlevé ou trop court.

5 *GROOMING AND SHOW PRESENTATION*

There is a vast selection of grooming equipment for the Bichon Frisé to choose from these days. The basic tools are a pair of the best long-bladed barber's scissors you can afford, and a pair with a short blade. A pair of curved scissors can also be useful. Then you will need a bristle brush, one large slicker brush and a small one; these should be soft and well-padded. Next on the list are nail clippers and a nail file, a tooth scaler, and a selection of steel combs with both close and wide-set teeth.

To dry the coat there is a variety of driers. You will need a high-velocity model, to remove excess water quickly, before using a drier with a selection of speeds and temperatures, in combination with a slicker brush, when straightening the coat before trimming.

The Bichon's coat is dense and soft, and very curly if left to dry naturally.

However, for the show ring, the coat is brushed and blow-dried, then combed and scissored to produce the 'powder puff' effect.

As scissoring can both improve and enhance the Bichon's outline, before you start trimming, study your dog's outline. If it looks too long in back, do not make it look longer by leaving too much hair on the chest and rump. If the dog is too short on leg, trim the hair shorter under the body and at the top of the leg.

Have a photo of a well-presented Bichon to study while you work. The use of a large mirror, set up at a distance, in which you can study the dog's outline, is also a great help.

It is important that the Bichon's coat is combed through to remove all mats before bathing; once they are wet they are impossible to remove without cutting.

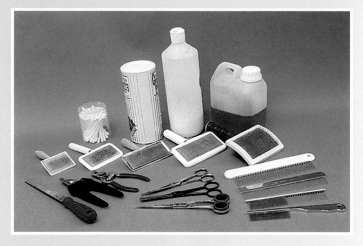

Grooming and Bathing equipment required for the Bichon Frisé.

Photo: Marc Henrie.

BATHING
Photos: Marc Henrie, Groomer Yvette Caunter.

1. Unwashed and untrimmed.

2. Using a rubber mat, place the dog in the bath after inserting cotton-wool (cotton) in both ears.

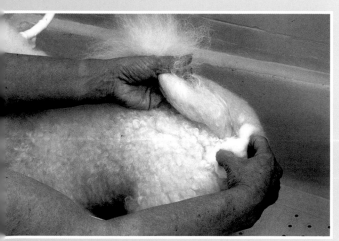

3. Clearing the anal glands; there is one on each side of the anus.

4. Check the temperature of the water – it should be hand-hot.

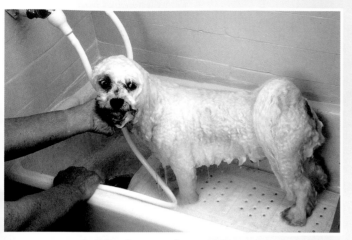

5. Wet the coat thoroughly.

6. Using a diluted blue shampoo, pour it on the coat.

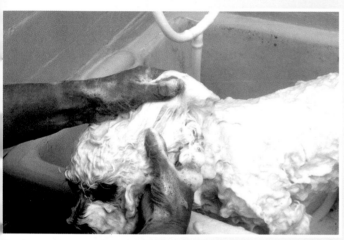

7. Take care when lathering near the eyes. It is a good idea to use a baby shampoo around this area. Hold the ear when washing the leathers.

8. Lather the coat thoroughly all over, not forgetting the legs, feet and tail.

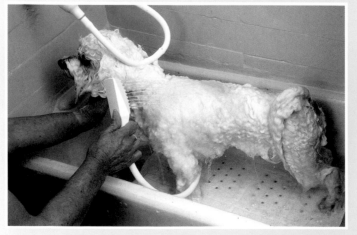

9. It is important that all shampoo is rinsed from the coat. Rinse until the water is quite clear. Any residue left behind leaves the coat dull.

BATHING

10. *Protect the eyes when rinsing the head.*

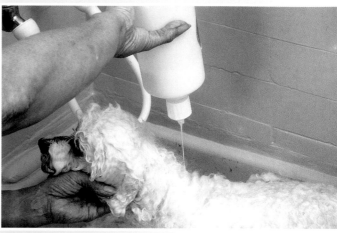

11. *Now use the conditioner.*

12. *Work the conditioner all through the coat, then rinse thoroughly.*

13. *Note the tight corkscrew curls.*

14. *Wrap the dog in a warm towel and remove the cotton-wool (cotton) from the ears.*

BRUSHING THROUGH THE WET COAT
(Not all groomers consider this necessary.)
Photos: Marc Henrie.

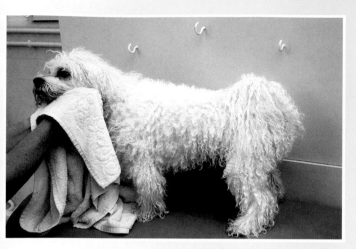

1. *Remove as much surplus water as possible.*

2. *With the large slicker brush start with the tail.*

3. *Using the slicker brush, go through the wet coat all over the body.*

4. *Hold the leg while using the brush.*

5. *Hold the ears to brush over and under the leathers.*

6. Hold the head while brushing the beard and muzzle.

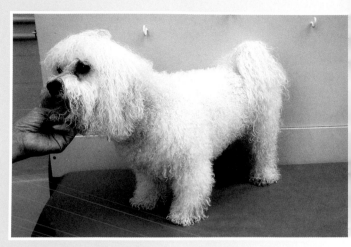

7. Still damp, showing the natural curl.

8. A powerful high-velocity drier is used to remove excess water; it does not dry the coat.

9. Lifting the leg to reach the pads.

10. Holding dog up makes it easy to reach under the body.

11. The tail: Here the groomer is using a slicker brush – I personally prefer a bristle-brush as the tail hair is long and quite silky.

12. Lift leg to blow underneath.

13. Hold muzzle while dealing with topknot.

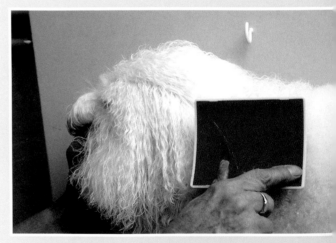

14. If the coat dries too quickly, respray with water before blow-drying.

15. Hold head down to blow-dry head and neck coat.

TRIMMING: STAGE I
Photos: Marc Henrie.

1. Now the Bichon is completely dry and ready for trimming. A restricting lead, as shown, can be useful. Always comb up the hair before scissoring.

2. Thinning the coat under the ears.

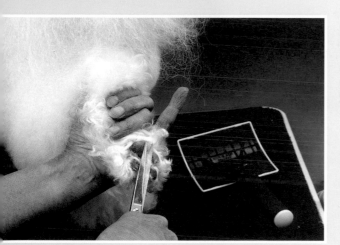

3. Hold the leg up to trim under the feet.

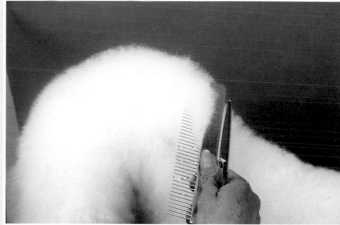

4. Combing through the coat prior to trimming.

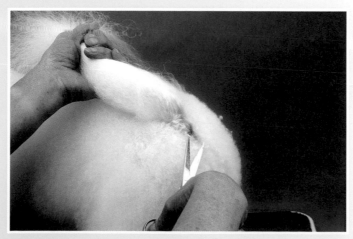

5. Hold the tail when scissoring under and around the anus.

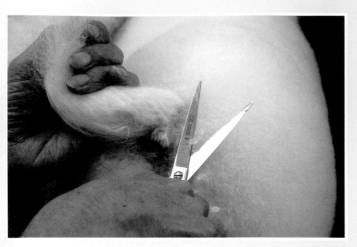

6. Note the position of the scissors.

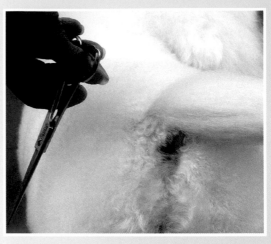

7. Scissoring the side of the leg.

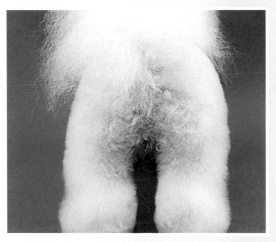

8. The finished rear quarters – a straight-sided upside-down U.

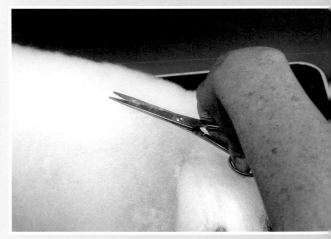

9. Always use scissors parallel to the body.

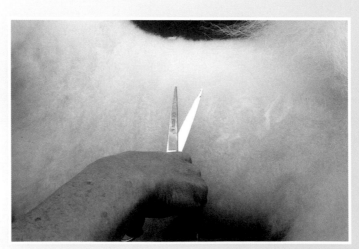

10. Trimming the side of the body.

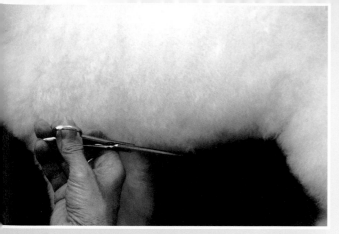

11. *Trimming down the side and under the body. Curved scissors can be useful here.*

12. *Hold the leg to comb and scissor as shown.*

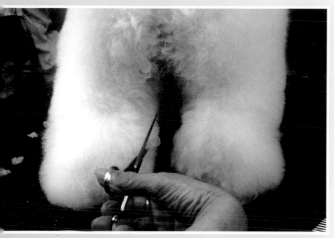

13. *Shape the inside of the leg with the dog standing.*

14. *The coat must be combed constantly while you are trimming.*

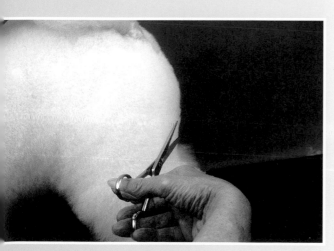

15. *Shaping the rear quarters.*

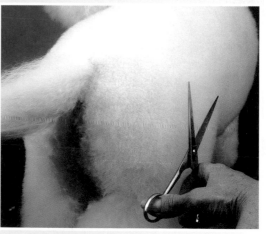

16. *The final light trimming to obtain that plush effect.*

TRIMMING: STAGE II
Photos: Marc Henrie.

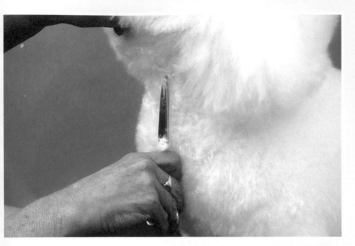

1. Hold the beard while trimming under the chin.

2. Rounding the coat on the legs.

3. Shaping the bottom of the leg around the pads.

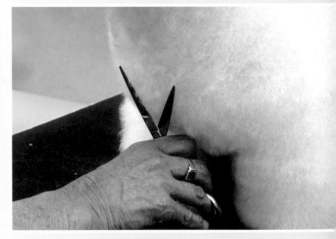

4. Blending the top of leg into the body coat.

5. Working on the side of the neck under the ear leathers.

6. Removing excess hair from ears with fingers or blunt tweezers, a little at a time.

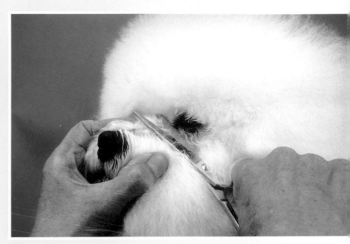

7. Hold the muzzle firmly while removing hair from inside the corner of the eyes with blunt-ended scissors. Keep the scissor-ends pointing away from the eyes.

8. Still holding the muzzle, firmly trim across the muzzle.

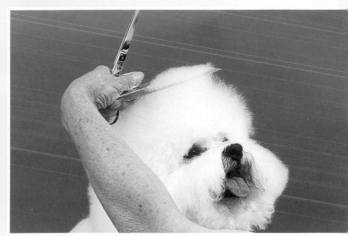

9. Comb the topknot and the hair over the eyes.

10. Hold the muzzle and trim over the eyes.

11. The shape of the topknot.

12. Shaping the beard to blend with the ear furnishings.

13. Finishing the topknot.

14. Shaping the neck.

15. Honeylyn Oo La La: Ready for the show ring.

Photo: Martin Leigh.

6 *THE SHOW RING*

I have owned pet dogs since I was very young, but in my early days the only dog show I had ever heard about was the Crufts Dog Show, and that did not mean very much to me.

When I was first introduced to the pedigree-dog scene I was astonished to learn that, on almost every weekend of the year, dog shows were being held – and this level of activity occurs in almost every country with a population interested in breeding and showing pedigree dogs.

THE PUPPY'S FIRST SHOW
When your puppy is six months of age, and providing he is happy and outgoing, looks in first-class condition with a fairly good coat, has learnt to walk well on the lead and has mastered the rudiments of show training (see Chapter Seven) and even more important, conforms to the Breed Standard in most respects, the time has

come to start thinking about entering him in a few shows. Choose a show fairly close to where you live, thereby avoiding a long journey which can be tiring for a young puppy.

THE SCHEDULES
Shows are advertised well in advance so there is plenty of time to phone or write to the Secretary for a schedule. This schedule contains a descriptive definition of classes, an entry form and the names of all breeds and the classes allocated to them. The schedule nearly always gives a map to enable you to find the venue; shows are often held in rather remote areas, so a map can be very useful. On receipt of the schedule choose which class or classes you wish to enter. With a puppy it is best not to tire him too much, so one or two classes such as Puppy and/or Novice are usually considered enough. In the US, a schedule is known as a 'premium list'. It includes the same information about the

show, and is usually available from the show superintendent, whose name can be obtained from the AKC.

THE ENTRY FORM
Fill in the entry form with care, enclose the right entrance fee and send it back to the secretary or superintendent before the closing date, which is printed on the front of the schedule. Always make a note of the classes you have entered. It is easy to forget those details, especially when you enter several shows at the same time, which can happen at the busiest time of the year when shows come in rapid succession. Make a special note if you enter more than one dog.

THE SHOW BAG
Keep a special bag or case for all the items needed at the show. You will need a benching blanket if you are attending a benched show, and a small water bowl. It is a good idea to take your own water with you, as this is the water your puppy is used to and so it is another precaution against upset stomachs. You will need a show lead – a nylon show lead is best for the Bichon Frisé, but if your puppy has been used to a leather collar and lead, use it for the first few shows, then gradually get him used to a nylon lead. You will need grooming equipment, a comb, a brush, scissors and grooming powder, as well as treats, kitchen towel, plastic bags to remove any excreta, and rubber bands to secure the same. You will need a clip to hold your ring number which is given to you when you enter the ring. A flask of coffee and a box of sandwiches complete the list.

The schedule, which may include the route to the show, your passes and ring numbers if sent, should be kept in another bag, or in a separate compartment in the show bag, as you will need them at the entrance to the show.

Ch. Pengorse Felicity of Tresilva (Leijazulip Giobertie – Tresilva Marianne).

Photo: Marc Henrie.

BE PREPARED

Be prepared for all types of weather. Most seasoned exhibitors keep in their cars everything for wet or dry, hot or cold weather, especially for the outdoor shows.

The Bichon Frisé always shows up better against dark-coloured clothing. Full flowing skirts will detract from the dog; close-fitting slacks or skirts are better. High-heeled shoes are a menace – indoors they make a loud noise and can frighten other dogs, out-of-doors they sink in the ground. Flat shoes are far more suitable for every occasion.

The Bichon Frisé, being a very intelligent dog, will know as soon as the day arrives that there is excitement in the air, so do try not to rush. Get up early, giving yourself time to follow your normal routine and load the car, thereby giving the puppy plenty of time to relieve himself before setting off on the journey.

AT THE SHOW

Catalogues are usually on sale at the entrance to the show, which can be quite a distance from your bench, so get a copy when you arrive. Find your bench. Although Bichons are supplied with cages at the Championship shows, often at other shows you will find either a bench or cage with your number on. Make the bench or cage comfortable with the blanket and secure the puppy either by his lead, which must not be too long, or, if a cage is provided, close the door and fasten it securely. An added protection is to tie the lead around the door. Benching or cages are quite often not used at shows. If that is the case, find a spot to settle in and make sure it is not too far from your ring.

Once you have unpacked and have set up your grooming table in the area provided, take the puppy for a slow walk around the show ground, giving him time to become acclimatised to the general noise and atmosphere. It is a good idea to find where the ring allocated to your breed is situated.

THE JUDGING

When your class is called, go into the ring quietly. If you get nervous you will communicate this to the puppy, so, no matter how you feel, stay as calm as possible.

As soon as judging commences set your puppy up in the correct position as practised at home, listen to the judge, move as the judge requests and stay in the position you are directed to.

Once the judge has selected his winners, if you are not among them congratulate the winner and leave the ring quietly. Whether you win or lose, praise your dog; he will have done his best to please you.

The first shows are always somewhat overwhelming to both puppy and owner, but at these shows you will be able to learn many things from other exhibitors and will, in addition, enjoy a day among other people dedicated to the Bichon Frisé.

SYSTEMS OF JUDGING

Although the principles remain the same – that dogs are judged against the appropriate Breed Standard, and the dogs placed in order of merit – at dog shows around the world there are different systems to be found.

THE FCI SYSTEM

The Fédération Cynologique Internationale, an umbrella organisation of which all the European countries, and many more, are members suggests, for example, that dogs are first quality-graded and then those given the top grading compete for the placings in each of the classes. This can be confusing to foreign visitors, as when a Scandinavian exhibitor says that his dog has won a "First" this may mean simply a First grading (or Excellent if you happen to be in another country). This means that the dog is considered an excellent example of its breed with no serious faults. Those dogs which have obtained First gradings will then compete for the placings, and a further honour can be obtained if they receive a Certificate Quality grading.

Most of the FCI member countries

also employ a system by which the judge gives each dog judged a detailed written critique, which is very helpful to the exhibitors, the breed clubs, and the judges themselves.

From the dogs graded Certificate Quality, the winners of the various certificates will be determined. This again may be confusing to the uninitiated, as it is not necessarily the best dog which receives the certificate! FCI rules dictate that dogs have to be of a certain age before they can win Certificates, and then when they have won so many, they can win no more, so it is quite feasible for, say, the dog standing Third in the Best Dog challenge to win an International Certificate, if the Best Dog is too young and the Second Best has already gained its International Title.

THE UK SYSTEM

The British system is much more straightforward, as the best dog (in the opinion of the judge on the day) always wins the Challenge Certificate. The only restriction is that, to become a Champion, a dog must have won three CCs under three different judges, and at least one of these should be won when the dog is over a year old.

TYPES OF SHOW

In the UK there a four different types of show – Championship, Open, Limited and Exemption. I will try to explain the differences between them.

Only the Championship Shows award the KC Challenge Certificates – CCs. At the Championship Shows you will see all the very best of British dogs, therefore the competition is very keen. Many exhibitors will have travelled

Ann Halliwell's Ch. Roxara He Drives You Wild (Eng. Aus. Ch. Charnel Born to be Wild About Roxara – Vythea Jump for Joy Around Roxara), handled by Marita Rodgers. In a six-month period, this dog won 8 CCs, 8 BOBs, 7 Toy Groups, Pet Plan Junior Dog of the year, 2nd Top Toy Dog and 8th Top Dog of the Year All breeds. A spectacular achievement for any breed. Photo: Carol Ann Johnson.

many miles to be there, often leaving home in the middle of the night. All exhibitors enter these Shows with the expectation that their dog will be selected for a prize, therefore most

exhibitors do become rather tense. This is especially so while the judging is in progress – everyone is hoping for a CC.

The Open Shows are far less stressful and therefore very enjoyable. Although classes for Bichons may not be scheduled, there is usually an Any Variety Toy Breed class. These AV classes are ideal for a puppy needing to become acquainted with other breeds. Most Open Shows schedule classes for Bichons.

Limited Shows are run by Breed Clubs and are quite small affairs as they are limited to 75 classes and Champions are not allowed to enter. This type of show is ideal for puppies.

Lastly there are the Exemption Shows, usually held for a charity. These are also ideal for training young puppies.

The Exemption Shows are the only ones where a non-pedigree dog can be shown, which makes them popular with pet owners. In addition to the novelty classes, four classes are scheduled for pedigree dogs. Dogs can be entered on arrival at this type of show.

Until you have gained experience, it is wise to restrict your entries to the smaller shows where the atmosphere is relaxed and, as the competition is not so fierce, the exhibitors are far friendlier – some of them, like you, will be newcomers to the dog scene as well.

There is one other type of show. Most breed clubs hold a Championship Show and an Open Show once a year. This type of show is restricted to one breed, for example the Bichon Frisé. Young puppies and newcomers to the breed are always welcome.

Fanciers in the UK will find announcements giving the date, the venue, the names of the judges, the breeds and the classes for all forthcoming shows in the two weekly dog papers, *Dog World* and *Our Dogs*. Both these papers have columns written by experts specialising in all breeds recognised by the KC. These breed notes help to keep owners up to date with the various activities and matters of interest pertaining to their breed.

BECOMING A CHAMPION

For a dog to gain the title of Champion in England is a much more difficult feat than in any other country. To become a Champion in most other countries is relatively easy, and in some countries a dog can attain the title of Champion without ever meeting another dog.

To start with, the numbers of class entries at the Championship shows in the UK are far higher than those of other countries, consequently the competition is far greater. The quality in the classes in the USA is often quite high but there is one vital difference: once a dog gains its American status as Champion it is usually no longer in competition with those dogs who are still chasing their title. American Champions are restricted to entering either in Open or in a class scheduled

for Champions only. In the USA, showing a Champion in the Open class is frowned upon and is almost never done. Much the same system, with slight variations, occurs in Scandinavia and on the Continent.

In the UK once a dog is a Champion it can and usually does continue to compete in the Open class for as long as the owner wishes. Consequently a really outstanding dog can gain many CCs, thus preventing others from achieving their title.

During the period of time that the breed record holder Ch. Sibon Fatal Attraction at Pamplona was exhibited she won 30 CCs; therefore only one other bitch became a Champion during that time.

Sue Dunger's Ch. Happy Hurbert.

To have bred a Champion, or better still several Champions, is always a great thrill and sense of achievement, as the breeder will be aware that his or her breeding programme is moving in the right direction.

The KC rules for Champions require a dog to win three Challenge Certificates under three different judges. If these three CCs are won before the dog is a year old, then one more CC must be won after the puppy's first birthday, before the dog can be awarded the title of Champion. This is because young puppies can change as they reach maturity, and not always for the best.

Reserve CCs are awarded to the dog the judge considers the next best dog to the CC-winner. In the event of the CC-winner being disqualified, the Reserve dog will automatically be awarded the CC.

ALLOCATION OF CCs

The Bichon Frisé was first granted Championship status in the UK in 1980. The allocation of Challenge Certificates (CCs) varies according to the number registered with the KC and the average number of Bichons attending Championship shows.

Champions are usually shown for as

Three Champions from the Bobander kennels of Chris Wyatt. Pictured (left to right): Ch. Bobander Secret in the Air, Ch. Bobander What Ho Bertie, and Ch. Bobander Spring in the Air.

long as they continue to look in first-class condition, but they should not be exhibited again under a judge that has already awarded them a CC. The one exception to this unwritten rule is at Crufts, which is understandable.

During 1980 and 1981 Bichons were awarded only six sets of CCs, six for dogs and six for bitches. In 1982, with the increase in registrations, the breed's allocation increased to 11 sets.

These three years produced nine English Champions, five dogs and four bitches. Four of the first male Champions, whose influence on the breed is largely responsible for the success of the Bichon in Britain, were sired by dogs from European bloodlines. The allocation of CCs has risen steadily over the years.

JUNIOR WARRANT

This is a special Kennel Club award for young dogs who have obtained 25 points between the ages of six and 18 months. This award has recently been upgraded, with the added kudos that once a dog has gained the required 25 points, in addition to being allowed to add the initials JW after the dog's name on pedigrees, on entry forms and in catalogues, the dog will now be allocated a KC Stud Book number.

A minimum of 12 points must be won at Championship Shows where CCs are on offer and 12 points won at Open Shows or Championship Shows without CCs on offer.

Points are awarded as follows:

At Championship Shows with CCs on offer for the breed, 3 points for a first prize.

At Championship shows without CCs and at Open Shows, 1 point for a first prize.

Points cannot be claimed unless there are a minimum of three dogs present in these classes.

There is one other stipulation. There must be three clear days between shows; in other words if you won at a show held on Saturday, that would count, but any wins on the following three days would not. This last requirement is to prevent owners rushing around the country at weekends which would be both tiring and stressful for young dogs. A Junior Warrant is by no means easy to acquire and it is quite an achievement

THE AMERICAN SYSTEM

The American system is in some ways very straightforward, but even then it has its complexities.

Whereas in Britain we have Championship shows, Open shows and Limited shows, most of the shows in the US are actually Points shows (Championship shows), though there are also "Match shows" which can be likened to the Open events in Britain. These are used by exhibitors mainly for accustoming young dogs to the show ring and are quite relaxed events.

Another point where the larger

Showing in the USA: This is Ch. Alpenglow Ashley Du Clamour, No. 1 Bichon, No.1 Non Sporting dog, and National Specialty Show winner for 1988.
Bred by Linda Day and Barbara Stubbs, owned by Lois Morrow.

Photo: Michele Perlmutter.

American shows and those in Britain and Europe differ is that many of the dogs are shown by professional handlers. Oftentimes a dog in the United States will be shown by its owner at smaller shows and breed specialties, but if it shows great promise it will be put in the hands of a professional handler who will travel great distances with it and campaign it far and wide. This can be an expensive business, and so breeders may be forced to find wealthy co-owners who will help finance their dog's show career. It is not unusual in the States to find dogs which have as many as six co-owners, each of which contributes to its campaign. Much expense is incurred with advertising the top winning show dogs in countless specialist magazines, and this item alone can demand a budget of thousands of dollars per year.

BECOMING A CHAMPION
To become a Champion in the US requires the dog to win 15 points, including two "majors" (which must be of 3, 4 or 5 points) under at least three different judges. There is no age restriction on a dog becoming an American Champion, and many "finish" their title as very young puppies.

The schedule of points in the US is quite complex. It is based on a mathematical formula that is applied to the actual dogs in competition within each sex of each breed, in each of the nine divisions in the continental US. It is calculated on a three-year basis.

The total number of shows where there was competition for a sex of a particular breed is taken, and the schedule for the following year is calculated so that as close as possible to 18 per cent of these shows may be expected to draw 3, 4 or 5 point entries. The entries at both Specialty and all-breed shows are considered, although rotating national specialty shows are deleted from the calculation.

The projected schedule is based upon regular class competition only. Thus, if additional majors are created as a result of dogs going Best of Winners, Best of Breed or Best Opposite Sex, these are not considered in the calculations for future schedules.

There are so few shows in Alaska, Hawaii and Puerto Rico that these points schedules are calculated manually. Here it is a matter of ensuring majors in those areas, and also of taking steps to try to ensure that every show will not carry major points for a sex of a breed.

No dog can win more than five points at any one show, but it is quite feasible for a dog to finish its title on three consecutive days, as many American shows are staged in clusters, with several shows being held in the same area over several consecutive days.

Once a dog has won its Championship title in the United States, it can then be automatically transferred into the Best of Breed class which is restricted to Champions. In essence, this means that the big difference between American shows and others is that a dog can win its Championship by beating only the non-Champions in its breed and sex, so it is obviously easier to become a Champion in the US than in Britain.

THE CLASSES

The classes which are on offer, prior to the Best of Breed class, for each sex are as follows:

Puppy: 6 to 9 months, or 9-12 months and 12-18 months – self explanatory.

Novice – For dogs which have never won a blue ribbon (first) in any of the other classes, or have won less than three firsts in the Novice class.

Bred by Exhibitor: The exhibitor is also the breeder.

American-Bred: The dog's parents were mated in America and the dog was born in America.

Open: any dog of that breed.

After these classes are judged, all the dogs that won first place in the classes compete again to decide the best of the winning dogs. This also is done separately for male and female dogs. Only the best male (Winners Dog) and the best female (Winners Bitch) receive Championship points. A Reserve Winner award is given in each sex to the runner-up.

The Winners Dog and Winners Bitch then go on to compete with the Champions for the title of Best of Breed. Three awards are usually given:

Best of Breed: the dog judged as the best in its category.

Best of Winners: the dog judged best between the Winners Dog and Winners Bitch.

Best of Opposite Sex: the best dog of the opposite sex to the Best of Breed winner.

Only the Best of Breed winners advance to compete in the Group competition. The Bichon Frisé is classified in the Non Sporting Group in the USA whereas in the UK it appears in the Toy Group. Again a point of confusion arises in the colours of American ribbons as opposed to British rosettes. In the UK, first prize receives a red rosette (when they are offered), second blue, third yellow, and reserve (fourth) green. Fewer and fewer UK shows now offer rosettes, and it is not obligatory to offer them.

However, in the US ribbons must be awarded (when the judge feels the dogs merit it) as follows:

Blue – for first place in any regular class. Also awarded to the winner of each group competition, usually in a rosette form.

> Red – for second place as above.
> Yellow – for third place as above.
> White – for fourth place as above.
> Purple – awarded to the Winners Dog and Winners Bitch.

Since these are the classes in which Championship points are earned, they are highly prized.

> Purple and White – awarded to the Reserve Winners Dog and Reserve Winners Bitch.
> Blue and White – awarded to the Best of Winners.
> Purple and Gold – awarded to the Best of Breed.
> Red and White – awarded to the Best of Opposite Sex.
> Red, White and Blue (or the colours of the show-giving club) – awarded only to the Best in Show.

THE YOUNG EXHIBITOR

There is increasing importance being placed on the role of Junior enthusiasts, both in the UK and in the US. For many young people between the ages of eight and eighteen the formation of the Kennel Club Junior Organisation provided a vehicle for young enthusiasts to become involved with all aspects of dog showing, and many shows schedule classes for their members. This organisation was founded to promote sportsmanship, courtesy, loyalty and self-discipline among young devotees of the dog, and it offers the opportunity to any young person, whether they own a dog or not, to join in the various interesting activities held during each year. These can either be regular classes, where the quality of the dog is assessed, or handling classes, where the quality of the dog is ignored, as only the ability of the handler is considered.

By joining the KCJO youngsters are able to enjoy many activities connected with the dog world, including visits to shows, dog training centres, dog trials, local kennels, dog sanctuaries and various other activities, all enjoyable. If so desired it is possible to learn about the care and training of the dog from experts such as veterinary surgeons, training instructors, and, of particular interest to the Bichon owner, canine beauticians.

During the holiday periods Agility and Obedience competitions are held with an annual quiz competition to find

The final of the Junior Handling Association, 1994 . The winner was Tamara Dawson with Ch. Tamalva Keep the Faith for Mistama. Tamara won this competition two years running.

the winning regional team. Every year many of the great Championship Shows schedule KCJO Any Variety (any Breed) Stakes classes confined to members. These are classes for members to show their dogs. In the KCJO classes the dogs are judged, not the handlers.

One other interesting yearly occasion is the competition for "Junior of the Year" based on an original written and pictorial "Project and Diary of all the Canine activities of the Year". The winner of this competition is awarded the Shaun McAlpine Memorial Trophy normally presented at Crufts.

In addition, the Junior Handling Association in the UK, founded by Joe Cartledge among others, provides qualifying heats at many shows which allow successful Juniors to compete at the Semi-Finals, held at Richmond Championship show in September. Here each of the seven groups produce winners from two different age groups who then compete at the Finals the following January, to find the overall winner.

An International Junior Handling Final is always held at Crufts show where national winners from all over the world compete. This is quite a spectacular event.

In the USA one of the highlights of the famous Westminster show is the

"Junior Showmanship" competition. As would be expected, the level of professionalism found here is quite remarkable, where many sophisticated youngsters, immaculately turned out, belie their years by their abilities.

Also, in the US, judges need to be approved by the American Kennel Club before they can judge Junior Showmanship classes, whereas in the UK anyone can officiate in this capacity.

Juniors are judged on their ability to present and handle their dogs within the same formats and guidelines as those who compete in the regular breed ring. The quality of their presentation, not the dog, is judged. Juniors are encouraged to develop their handling abilities, dress appropriately, conduct themselves in a proper manner and present their dog in a well-groomed condition.

Due to the large number of professional or semi-professional handlers in the US, there is a great opportunity for keen young people to apprentice themselves to an established handler during their school holidays, and many seize this chance. Oftentimes those who have done so, and enjoyed and learnt from the experience, choose to follow this path as a career and there are many opportunities to do so. Many of the leading handlers today started out as assistants to the great handlers, many of whom subsequently retired and became judges, and while it is a career which demands incredibly hard work, it brings great rewards, both financially and in the satisfaction it brings from getting the very best out of their charges.

The level of presentation seen in the United States is quite remarkable, and

Joan Gadd Davies' Ch. Tresilva Snowdon of Suanalu.

many handlers' assistants achieve an amazingly high level in this field. Much emphasis is placed on grooming in the American show ring, and it is unlikely that you will ever witness an ill-prepared dog at an American show. Learning the art – and it is an art – comes more easily to some young people than others, and invariably it is those who have the "gift" who will rise to the top.

For those who are prepared to dedicate their lives to a life on the road, and much hard work at home, a career in handling can prove very worthwhile in the States.

JUDGING THE BICHON FRISE

The judging system in Britain is such that judges can only come forward for Kennel Club approval when they have received an invitation to judge the breed at a Championship show. They will be required to complete a detailed questionnaire which will be referred to the breed clubs, and then the Kennel Club Judges Committee will make a recommendation to the General Committee that the judge concerned be approved or otherwise.

In the United States, would-be judges can apply to the American Kennel Club. Again their experience will be considered and they will be given a provisional judging licence, if successful, for that breed. After having completed several assignments they may be licensed, and then are free to apply for further breeds.

DO YOU QUALIFY?

By making the wrong decisions, judges can do untold harm to a breed, so it is very important that dogs are placed according to their merit. Judging requires a thorough understanding of a dog's anatomy and structure, a sound knowledge of the Breed Standard, and integrity with impartiality. Judges are there to select the best specimen in type and quality for the award of BOB, without any regard for the handler on the other end of the lead.

Before you accept any invitation, you must be confident of your own ability to recognise "type" and that you know how to interpret and understand the Standard. Judges should also understand the national governing body's rules and regulations. A good memory is also essential. Judges need to recall the faults and virtues of every dog in each class. The judge might forget an obvious fault but the spectators at the ring side will not, and an inferior standard of judging will not go unnoticed or be forgotten.

THE INVITATION

Quite often invitations are first issued verbally, probably at a show. This will be followed by a written invitation from the Club's Secretary. Sometimes you may be asked to judge in an honorary capacity, or the society may ask if any expenses are required.

Make sure you keep accurate records of all judging appointments as they will

Top international judge Ferelith Somerfield at the Bichon Frisé Club of Great Britain.

Photo: Marc Henrie.

be required by the authorities when you eventually receive an invitation to award Championship points. Judging records must give the name and date of the show, the number of dogs entered, the number of dogs judged, plus the number of absentees.

Dress with care. At an outside show, do not wear a flowing skirt which may blow over the dog's faces if it is windy; do not wear dangling jewellery, and men should avoid ties which flap. I have found it unwise to wear any perfume. A dog's nose is very sensitive to distracting odours, and nobody appreciates a dog jumping up to get a better smell.

IN THE RING

Judges should arrive at the show at least half an hour before judging commences. Report to the show secretary, who will supply you with the judge's badge and your judging book. Go to your allocated ring ten minutes before judging is due to start. Greet your stewards and tell them where you wish the new dogs, and the seen dogs from previous classes, to stand.

As the steward calls the dogs into the ring, sit quietly until the class is ready, then walk down the line of dogs studying each one, then ask the exhibitors to walk their dogs round the ring once. This will help the dogs to settle and will give you the chance to get a general idea of the quality in the class.

Heavily-coated dogs like the Bichon Frisé are more difficult to judge than the smooth-coated breeds. When judging smooth-coated dogs most of the anatomy can be seen and assessed without using your hands. With the Bichon's dense coat, it is possible to hide many faults – so many facets can be scissored to give a false impression. Therefore, it is essential that judges use their hands to assess important requirements in the Standard.

Do not start examining any dog until the owner has stacked the dog to his or her satisfaction and is holding him steady by the lead. Just stand well back and assess the dog's overall balance.

The first class of the day is always traumatic. Apart from you being nervous, especially if it is your first appointment, the first class is usually a

Puppy class which can be difficult. When judging puppies always make allowances. A Bichon puppy should never be penalised for playing around. Our Standard calls for a 'gay, happy, lively little dog' which I personally like to see in the youngsters.

THE EXAMINATION

Start your examination from the front. Gently lift the lips to check that the bite is correct [scissor], examine the head and expression, note the colour [dark], size [fairly large], and shape [round], of the eyes, and check that the eyes are set forward-looking and fairly wide apart.

The required dark haloes and eye rims need to be checked; if they lack pigmentation, the Bichon's expression will be incorrect. Lift the ear leathers, look for the correct ear-set and length of the leathers.

However, the shape of the skull [only very slightly rounded], the width of the zygomatic arch [wide not flat], the length of the skull from stop to occiput [ratio of muzzle length to skull length 3:5], all these important points are completely hidden by the Bichon's thick dense coat and can only be assessed by using the hands. If the head is of the correct width and length, lines drawn from the outer corners of each eye to the tip of the nose will create an equilateral triangle; in other words the measurements from corner to corner and from corner to tip of nose should be the same.

Nose [large round, black and shiny]. A nose lacking in pigment is a serious fault.

The length of neck [fairly long]. The Bichon's coat [fine silky and curly] can be cleverly scissored to give an illusion of length, a high top-knot of hair gives the impression of a good reach of neck. Only by feeling under the coat can the length of neck be truly assessed.

To ascertain the following points you must use your hands. Lay-back of shoulder [oblique, not prominent], length of upper arm [equal in length to shoulder], the bone [not too fine], bend of stifle [well bent], the spring of rib

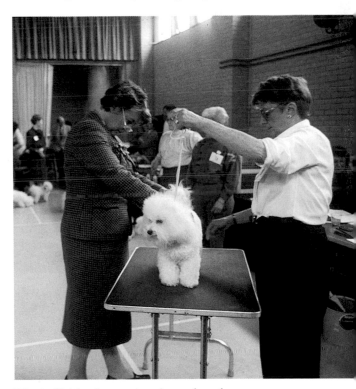

The individual examination takes place on the table.   *Photo: Marc Henrie.*

[well-sprung], correct topline and depth of brisket [deep]. Length from withers to tail-set should equal height from withers to ground.

A kink in the tail is undesirable, as is a tail touching the back, so do not forget to run your hand down its length, for the long coat completely hides a bent or kinked tail. If the dog is male, do not forget to check that he is entire.

The overall balance of the Bichon Frisé is fairly easy to see but even this can be improved by clever scissoring. It is therefore very important that all who judge this breed have used their hands before making their final decisions.

Only by close examination will a judge find the incorrect flat zygomatic arch proving that the skull is too narrow. By feeling an upright shoulder or a short forearm a judge will know, before the dog moves, that with these faults he will not move correctly, just as a dog lacking in angulation, with straight stifles or crooked hocks, cannot move soundly with drive. After examining each dog, ask the handler, politely, to move their dog in a triangle, then to walk the dog up and down in a straight line, to assess the movement.

Judge for Type, Balance, and Soundness, in that order. Type – a Bichon should look like a Bichon. Balance – an harmonious blending of all parts of the dog. Soundness – in both movement and temperament.

THE CRITIQUES

After judging, the most onerous necessity is the writing of a critique on the dogs you have judged. In most countries, a judge is required to write an immediate critique on every dog, but these critiques are only seen by the exhibitor and the appropriate kennel club. In the UK, a judge is expected to write a critique just on the first and second in every class at the Championship shows, on the first at Open shows, and at Crufts on the first, second and third in every class. These critiques are published in the two weekly dog papers.

When you make notes at the show, write down the faults not the virtues. It is impossible to remember every dog in detail but, by noting the faults, your critique will not contain any discrepancies. However, do not include these faults in the critique, this is merely an aide-mémoire. I prefer to leave other judges to find the faults themselves. A judge is there to judge the dog on the day.

7 *TRAINING YOUR BICHON*

Your puppy has always had the company of littermates and is quite unused to being alone, so we can understand how very strange and frightened he will feel on entering your home. The puppy must, however, quickly learn the rules of his new home.

The first things that the puppy must learn are to recognise and respond to his name and to be house-trained. Call the puppy the name you have chosen for him and give him a treat when he comes. Never call a puppy to administer discipline or for any other reasons he could find unpleasant while he is learning his name; it is important that the puppy should always associate hearing his name with enjoyable experiences.

HOUSE TRAINING

This requires much patience and observation on the owner's part. Puppies by nature have an instinct to be clean. They will never soil their sleeping area, which they will always leave if they wish to relieve themselves; so at the beginning paper should always be placed just outside your puppy's bed.

Puppies will always relieve themselves after a nap, so put your Bichon on to newspaper or, if the weather permits and he has been immunised, take him outside and stay with him until he does what is expected of him. Then praise him. All puppies respond to tone of voice and can quickly distinguish between pleasure and annoyance. While inside the house, always keep an eye on the puppy to avoid any mistakes. Puppies always circle round with their nose to the ground before relieving themselves. When you see this happening, quickly pick the puppy up and place him on the paper or in the garden, once again waiting with him until he has done what is required of him.

At first the newspaper should be placed fairly liberally around a small

Training should start as soon as your puppy arrives home.

Photo: Marc Henrie.

room with an easily cleaned floor. As time goes by, gradually decrease the amount but always leave the paper near the back door.

LEAD TRAINING

Although serious training should not start until the puppy is 12 weeks of age, he should get used to wearing a collar as soon as possible. A soft collar is preferable and as soon as the puppy gets used to the collar, lead training can commence.

Start lead training in the garden. Just attach the lead to the collar and let the puppy walk around the garden; do not restrict him, just let him wander. After a few minutes pick up the lead and gently pull the lead towards you, calling the puppy by name at the same time. He will probably start to pull and strain in the opposite direction at first. If this happens, drop the lead again and let the puppy wander around for a little while, then pick the lead up again and repeat the performance. As soon as the puppy comes when the lead is gently pulled, reward him with a treat and much praise. Never leave a puppy alone when he is wearing a collar, with or without the lead on it; both collar and lead can be dangerous if they get caught on any protruding object. With time and patience you will soon have a well-trained youngster.

SOCIALISATION

As soon as the puppy has received all his inoculations, it is important that he gets used to all the strange sights and sounds of the world outside his home.

From the very beginning, let all friends and visitors to your home make a fuss of the puppy. As soon as possible after the full course of inoculations has taken hold, take him for short walks in a busy street daily until the pup accepts the noise and bustle with confidence. Introduce your Bichon to as many new experiences as you can so he will grow into a well-rounded, totally self-assured companion.

Trips in the car should start at a very early age. In my experience, puppies taken in the car from eight weeks rarely suffer from car sickness when they are older.

BASIC OBEDIENCE

Six months is considered the right time for serious training, but it is my opinion that the earlier training starts, the easier it is to train a Bichon puppy which you intend to show. I start teaching the pup to stand on a table and to stay while his teeth are gently examined when he is between three and four months, but this decision is up to the owner.

The commands "Sit", "Down" and "Stay" are not required for a show dog, but are useful for the pet owner, so I will try to give brief instructions when and how to teach these commands to your Bichon.

Firstly, the most important aspect of training is that the trainer must have the utmost patience; it is a question of try and try again, but never sound cross or bad-tempered. Training must always be an enjoyable time for the puppy, and success must always be rewarded by a tidbit or praise and affection. Training sessions should be carried out by the same person, starting with short lessons of no more than ten minutes (any longer and the dog will get bored). These should be done little and often, at least twice a day. You will need a fairly long lead, about six feet in length, as the lead must be held in the right hand leaving your left hand free to control the lead and to help when giving commands such as Sit.

SIT

It is important that all training is carried out in a secluded area away from other sources of distraction. With the lead in your right hand, and the dog on your left, give the command "Sit". At the same time, place your left hand on the dog's hindquarters and press down gently keeping the lead taut with your right hand. As soon as the dog sits, give

Be firm, but tactful, and your puppy will soon understand what is required.

Photo: Marc Henrie.

a tidbit or lavish praise. Practise this routine until the dog sits on command without any pressure applied to his hindquarters and once again praise lavishly.

DOWN

To achieve the "Down" command, get the dog in the Sit position and give the "Down" command while gently pushing down on the withers with one hand and sliding the forelegs forward with the right hand until the dog's body is on the ground. Then signal with your hand (extend your arm with the palm of your hand facing the dog) and tell the dog that you want him to "Stay". Practise this until the dog goes down without any help.

STAY

Do not attempt the Stay command until the dog has learnt to sit on command. Once this is achieved, still with the lead in your right hand and the dog on your left, give the command "Sit" and move a little distance in front of the dog. Give the "Stay" hand signal (see above) with the "Stay" command. Repeat this instruction until the dog stays, and then gradually move even further away, repeating this exercise on the lead and eventually without the lead. Do not forget to reward your Bichon every time the exercise is successful.

POSITIVE THINKING

The commands that the dog has mastered must be repeated regularly – like humans, dogs can easily forget some of what is expected of them. The Bichon is a companion dog and quickly understands by your tone of voice whether he has pleased or annoyed you. Never physically punish a dog when he has done something wrong; let him know you are displeased just by tone of voice. You must also remember that you can only do this if you have caught him in the act – even five minutes later, he will not remember and so will not understand what he has done wrong.

COMPETITIVE OBEDIENCE

The three exercises above are fairly easy for the pet owner, but if anyone wants to train a dog for competition in the Obedience and Agility classes, I strongly recommend you join a local training class specialising in the many varied and complicated exercises required in serious competition. Your dog's breeder, your vet or your kennel club will know where the nearest class is held. Do not underestimate the Bichon's intelligence. From centuries of close association with people, Bichons are most intuitive and are quite capable of achieving a high standard of training.

Vera Goold of Leijazulip fame has trained several Bichons in Obedience at Open Shows in the UK, and she finds the breed a pleasure to work with, intelligent and very easily trained. Hopefully, if enough owners participate, the Bichon will do as well in Obedience

Ch. Cali-Col's Scalawag CD: 'High-scoring dog' winner at the first National Specialty 1976. Co-owned wih breeder Gertrude Fournier, Scally was trained and shown by Betty Ribble.

classes in the UK as he does in the USA and Australia.

When one thinks of Obedience, the breed that springs to mind is the Border Collie. Athletic, with an in-built need to work and to please, Border Collies excel as Obedience dogs. Bichons do not usually excel, but they enjoy having a go anyway. Jacqui McKenzie and her husband, Ron, who live in Suffolk, UK, were initially involved in Border Collie Obedience. However, the McKenzies relish a challenge and decided to train Bichons. They are hopeful that their promising dog, Jaunty James of High Trees, will have some Obedience success.

Jacqui believes Bichon Obedience training is simply a matter of containing the breed's natural effervescence and channelling it in the right direction. It is just as popular with the crowd as it is with the dogs: seeing a Bichon fetching a dumb-bell or doing heel-work in a Border Collie-dominated ring always amazes and delights the public.

By contrast, the American Bichons have been as successful in the Obedience ring as they have in the show ring. The Bichon Frisé Club of America has always supported these efforts by offering an Obedience Trial at every National Specialty. At the first Specialty, Ch. Cali-Col's Scalawag CD, co-owned and shown and trained by Betty Ribble for owner Gertrude Fournier, won High In Trial. As a retired show dog Scally proved he could perform in any venue.

Bichons have also achieved the highest award of accomplishment in Obedience competition by having more than one Obedience Trial Champion. This is a difficult title to acquire, as the dogs must frequently beat other OTCH dogs in order to win the points towards this title. Billijo Porter of Texas was the first to achieve this with her Bichon, C and D's B.A. Watson. Watson also won numerous High in Trials over some of the top Obedience dogs in the US.

Mrs Porter's next Bichon was Ch.

OTCH Sea Star's Sandpiper, UDX, NA. He won sixteen Highs in Trial and fourteen High Combined. Piper had the highest score ever earned by a Bichon, 199.5 out of a possible 200. In his spare time he was a licensed and working therapy dog, one of a very few allowed to work with paralysed and comatose patients.

AGILITY

Agility has been recognised by the AKC and this has become a marvellous arena for owners to enjoy their dogs, while the Bichons revel in the activity. A wide variety of small dogs take part in Mini-Agility in the UK, but it is not yet as popular as Standard Agility, and Bichons seem to be outnumbered by Jack Russells, Border Terriers and West Highland White Terriers. Apart from lower jumps, the course is the same as the Standard version, which can be a challenge for the owners. Because Bichons are so much smaller than, for example, a Border Collie, owners may initially have to stoop, while running the course, to be able to point to the obstacles and instruct their dogs. Owners who try their hands at Mini-Agility can take heart: Bichons are fairly quick learners, so putting up with a bad back should not be a problem for too long!

Am. Ch. OTCH Sea Star's Sandpiper UDX, NA competing in Agility. Owned and trained by Billijo Porter of Texas, USA.

*Am. Ch. Chaleen's Lochiel Chaminade TDI:
A Champion on the show ring, and now a
therapy dog who makes regular hospital visits
in Colorado, California.*

THERAPY DOGS

Eyes usually light up when a Bichon
visits a children's home, hospital,
hospice, or residential home. Cute,
brilliant white, soft and fluffy, Bichons
are just the right size to sit on a lap and
be fussed – and they love being the
centre of attention.

"They are popular because they are
good-natured, and very pretty dogs,"
says Pets As Therapy Dogs
administrator Frances Burtenshaw.
"They appeal to all age groups because
they are small enough to be put on the
laps of old people, and also to be
handled by young children, who may be
intimidated by larger dogs." There are
about 11,500 registered PAT Dogs in
the UK, with about 4,500 making

active visits. From this, there are 51
registered Bichon Frisés.

In the US, Bichons have also become
very active as therapy dogs, working in
facilities for children, the aged and
handicapped. These dogs are trained
and licensed before their work begins.
Many therapy dog organisations are
active around the US; however, a group
called 'Lend a Hand – Lend a Heart',
working in Northern California has
consistently had a large number of
Bichons in their programme.

TRAINING A SHOW DOG

I have explained the basics of lead
training earlier in this chapter, but in
addition to learning to walk on a lead, a
puppy needs to learn how to behave
and how to show him or herself to their
best advantage when in the show ring
in front of a judge.

A puppy must be trained to stand
quite still while the judge examines the
mouth and the body to assess the
conformation. He must learn to walk
beside his handler without pulling on
the lead and to learn to keep his head
held high – a dog sniffing the ground
will simply never look his best. He must
also learn how to walk in a triangle
pattern, how to change direction
smoothly, and to stand quite still when
the judge is making the final selection.

All this training is necessary as the
judge has very little time, only a little
more than two minutes, to examine and
watch how the dog stands and moves.

The polished show performer: Nick Skeet's Ch. My Leading Lady At Riordon.

Photo: David Dalton.

A restless dog that refuses to be examined will clearly be at a disadvantage in competition.

TONE OF VOICE

Dogs do not understand words, so it is important that you always use a different tone of voice when praising or reprimanding. To praise when the dog responds as desired, the voice should be soft and kind in tone; for making corrections, use a harsh and fairly loud tone. Dogs will quickly understand the difference between right and wrong by the sound of your voice.

In addition to praising your dog vocally, reward with a treat when your Bichon does what is required and the dog will soon learn what pleases or displeases you. You will never regret the amount of time and attention you give

to training a show prospect. Some dogs are natural performers and relish the atmosphere of the show ring; others need more 'bringing out'. All dogs, however, will benefit from a bit of polishing.

ON THE TABLE

Like almost all small breeds, the Bichon must always stand on a table for the judge's close examination. So, first and foremost, the puppy must be taught to stand quietly on the table in a show position while the judge examines his or her mouth and manually examines all parts of the dog's body, and if a male, the testicles. Table training should start at a very young age, the earlier the better.

Use a firm table with a non-slip surface. A puppy on a shaky or a

The Bichon puppy needs to be trained to stand on a table for inspection. Photo courtesy: Jackie Ransom.

slippery table will be frightened, especially at first when, without doubt, he will want to do everything except stand still. Always make sure he cannot jump or fall off the table by keeping one hand on the body. With the command 'stay' make him stand still for just a few seconds at first, gradually increasing the time so he stays still for at least a minute.

Practise this lesson several times a day, and do not forget to reward him with praise and a treat each time he remains quite still.

STAND AND STAY
Another lesson to be learnt by the puppy is to allow himself to be set in the best position to gain the judge's admiration. In order to place the front legs in their correct position, lift the head so the feet are just off the ground. As the head is released, the feet will come down quite parallel, with the feet turning neither in nor out. Next, place the rear legs so they are also parallel and not too close together. Then, with the collar placed just under the ears, hold the lead taut with one hand and with the other make sure the tail is kept curved over the back. Now give the command 'stay', and do not forget to give praise and reward.

THE BITE
It is always rather difficult to train any puppy to accept having his teeth examined. Judges need to open the mouth to check that the dog has the correct scissor bite. All dogs, unless trained when young, will resist whenever anyone tries to examine their mouths. Try getting as many of your friends as possible to look at your dog's teeth. It is not necessary to open the mouth; just lift the lips so the teeth can be seen. Say "teeth" each time you try doing this.

This lesson always seems to require more time and patience than any other, so when the puppy does let you look at his mouth without a struggle, reward with extra praise and a special treat.

THE WALK
When training a puppy to walk in a

The judge will assess overall conformation when the dog is gaited.

triangle pattern, turning smoothly on each change of direction, it is a good idea to fix up a square area in the garden where you can practise this routine as often as possible. When moving the puppy in a triangle, do turn slowly when you change direction, because any fast turn will alter the dog's stride, often causing him to hop; so give the dog time to change direction at his own speed. When practising the straight up-and-down, away from the judge and back again, remember to turn slowly.

The secret of training is short, frequent sessions, the use of the right tone of voice, the constant food rewards, and an endless supply of your patience.

Do remember when rewarding puppies for good behaviour with a variety of treats, that unless you take into account the quantity of food he has received in that way and deduct this amount from his daily diet, the puppy is likely to put on too much weight.

ADDITIONAL TRAINING
Ring Training Classes for a show prospect are well worth joining in order to get your puppy used to the noise and bustle of a dog show and the presence of other dogs of various shapes and sizes. They are also an additional help with your puppy's training. There is sure to be a class in your own vicinity. Ask local dog exhibitors, who will probably know where to find the nearest one. At these classes your puppy will be able to meet dogs both large and small of other breeds. The first sight of a giant dog must be quite frightening to small puppies. Ring Training or Ring Craft Classes are very friendly, casual affairs where you can socialise with other owners while getting your puppy trained.

8 BREEDING A LITTER

I have learnt from experience that breeding a litter of puppies can be expensive, time-consuming and often traumatic, so do consider carefully before embarking on such an enterprise.

It is my contention that the mating of dogs should be left in the hands of experienced breeders. Some understanding of the genetic background of both the sire and the dam make it possible for a breeder with experience, learnt over many years, to be reasonably sure that the results of such a mating will produce sound and healthy puppies.

There are many other factors affecting

The Nuage Bichons, owned by Bill Dreker in the USA.
Breeding is a complex business, and time should be spent researching pedigrees and gaining an understanding of basic genetics.

inheritance. Unwanted hidden recessives can lie dormant for many years before suddenly appearing in a litter when least expected.

If, however, a pet owner, or an exhibitor, intends to breed a litter in the hope of breeding a puppy of quality for future showing, I strongly advise that they go back to the breeder of their bitch for advice on the choice of the stud dog. The breeder should know from experience the best dog to suit your bitch.

Hereditary defects usually only appear in a proportion of a litter. Unscrupulous breeders can, therefore, do untold harm to a breed by exhibiting and breeding from the one dog from the litter who appears to be free of any of the defects carried by its siblings, although it may well be, and probably is, a carrier for the same defects.

The use of a top winning stud dog is not always the best choice, neither is your friend's pet dog.

GENETICS

This is a very involved and difficult subject and far beyond my capabilities to explain in any great depth. Many books have been written specialising in genetics, and these are well worth studying. I have listed the books I found easiest to understand in the bibliography at the end of this book. In the following notes I have tried to simplify what I have learnt about this very complicated subject.

All puppies receive 50 per cent of germ plasma from each parent; therefore researching into their background may be of some help towards the evaluation of the genetic patterns of any sire or dam you are considering using as a mate for your dog or bitch.

The dog's dominant traits can always be seen as he matures; the recessive, usually unwanted, traits will remain hidden.

THE GENES

There are two types of genes, the dominant and the recessive. The following list shows the desirable features we require in order to breed a Bichon of quality, conforming to the Breed Standard. You will note that these features come from both dominant and recessive genes.

A dominant gene can be lost. A recessive gene is never lost, the fault being carried unseen. For instance, if a dog and a bitch, both showing perfect bites but both carrying the hidden recessive gene responsible for an undershot jaw, are mated together, they could possibly produce, in a litter of four, at least one puppy showing this fault, while two of the puppies will be carriers and one puppy will be clear. However, this 1:2:1 is a ratio and works out only in large numbers of puppies produced over an extended period. Therefore the results of one litter cannot be taken as conclusive. This is one of the reasons why a recessive fault such as an undershot jaw is so difficult to eradicate.

DOMINANT TRAITS
- affect a large number of a dog's progeny.
- reduce any danger of continuing unwanted traits.
- are always visible in the dog.
- never skip a generation.
- will guarantee the breeding pattern.
- can be lost.

RECESSIVE TRAITS
- can, and often do, skip many generations.
- become apparent only when they are carried by both sire and dam.
- a puppy will exhibit the (usually) unwanted trait when it has two recessive genes, one inherited from the sire and one from the dam.
- a dog inheriting only one recessive gene will not show the trait.
- are never lost.

Therefore, if a dog carries a dominant gene, then that trait, whether a fault or a virtue, is always visible.

If a dog carries a recessive gene, the trait, whether for good or bad, is not always visible.

Most faults and defects in the dog are caused by unwanted recessive genes, although there are recessive genes required in some breeds. For example, an undershot mouth is required in the Tibetan Spaniel, as that breed's Standard calls for the mouth to be "slightly undershot". The white coat of the Bichon comes from a recessive gene.

As I mentioned before, I do not profess to be an authority on genetics but, from studying the many litters I have bred during the last 24 years, the following list of dominant and recessive traits, in my opinion, apply to the Bichon Frisé.

DOMINANT	RECESSIVE
Thick Coat	Sparse coat
Correct ears	Short ears
Low-set ears	High-set ears
Heavy bone	Fine bone
Large round eyes	Small eyes
Dark eyes	Light eyes
Deep chest	Shallow chest
Short muzzle	Long muzzle
Black solid pigment	White coat
Scissor bite	Undershot jaw/ overshot jaw

Recessive genes are responsible for the hereditary malformations and illnesses which are considered by the veterinary profession to be the most difficult to eradicate, due to the fact that these recessive genes are so often hidden, sometimes for many generations and will only crop up when both the sire and dam of a litter show themselves to be 'carriers'.

To summarise, if a dog carries a dominant trait this trait is always visible, but if a dog carries a recessive trait, this trait is not always visible; such a dog is a 'carrier'. The recessive trait will only become visible when puppies are produced from a mating to another 'carrier' – when the recessive gene is passed to the puppy from each parent.

RECESSIVE GENES

If two animals, both with correct dentition, are mated, producing a litter of four puppies and all four puppies have a correct, bite, it can be safely assumed that both their sire and dam are dominant for the correct dentition, but if one of the four pups' bite is incorrect, i.e undershot, both the sire and the dam are 'carriers' for the same recessive gene.

The litter of four puppies produced by two 'carriers' will result in one puppy being undershot, the three other puppies will all have correct bites, but two of the puppies will be 'carriers' for the recessive gene and one puppy will be clear .

The difficulty arises because, without a test mating, it is impossible to know which of the three puppies with the correct bite is the one that does not carry the recessive gene; but it is certain that their parents were both 'carriers'.

I hope this brief and elementary description of genetics will help Bichon breeders to understand that such faults as weak pigmentation can only be 'bred out' by using a dog known to be dominant for unbroken pigmentation.

A 'carrier' is quite useless. You may get a proportion of the puppies with solid pigment, but only one in four of the puppies proportionately will be dominant for solid pigmentation.

BREEDING SYSTEMS

There is more than one breeding method: there are three. These are in-breeding, line breeding and out-crossing.

IN-BREEDING

In-breeding is the mating of closely related animals such as father to daughter, son to mother, and the closest of all, brother to sister. Although this method has been successful in establishing many outstanding lines and many Champions, it is still viewed with suspicion. In-breeding does not produce any faults, it only shows up the faults already present in the genetic make-up of the closely related animals.

In-breeding is not the culprit if puppies are born with medical defects. It is the fault of uninformed breeders who, without the essential knowledge of the dogs' hereditary background, have used unsuitable animals.

In-breeding should not be practised by pet owners or novices. It is absolutely vital, when using this method, that the breeder knows the complete history and background of all the animals in the pedigrees of any dog or bitch intended for such a mating,

Any hereditary defect, be it a bad bite,

CH SULYKA PUZZLE
The sire is in the background of many top winning American Champions.

Leijazulip Guillaume
ENG & AUS CH Leijazulip Jazz of Zudiki
Ninon De La Buthiere of Leijazulip
ENG & IR CH Sulyka Snoopy
CH Leijazulip Kipling of Shamaney
Shamaney My Choice of Sulyka
Wentres Super Shelly
Puffin Billy of Sulyka

ENG & AUS CH Leijazulip Jazz of Zudiki
Vythea the Page Boy
Druidswood Blanchneige
Vythea Fragrance
Zudiki Charli Farli
Hunkidori Mischa
Cluneen Happy Heidi of Hunkidori

CH SULYKA PUZZLE

AUS CH Jazz De La Buthiere of Leijazulip
Leijazulip Guillaume
Leilah De La Buthiere of Leijazulip
ENG & AUS CH Leijazulip Jazz of Zudiki
INT CH Looping De La Buthiere
Ninon De La Buthiere of Leijazulip
FR CH Julia De La Buthiere

Fascination of Zudiki at Sulyka

Montravia Leander Snow Fox
Montravia Snow Demon
Montravia Leander Snow Princess
Petite White Velvet
Leander Snow Swept
Rownhams Snow Bird
Twinley Kisses of Rownhams

PENGORSE POLDARK *of* TRESILVA
Sire's pedigree of Breed Record Holder Ch Sibon Fatal Attraction at Pamplona

Ugo De Villa Sainval

INT CH Xorba De Chaponay

Quatna of Milton

Astor De Villa Sainval of Littlecourt

Vim De Villa Sainval

Yalta De Villa Sainval

Xophie De Villa Sainval

Leijazulip Benji

INT CH Racha De Villa Sainval

FR CH U Sam De Villa Sainval

Soraya De Villa Sainval

Leilah De La Buthiere of Leijazulip

BEL CH Nucky De Wanarbry

Tornado De La Buthiere

Rosy De La Roche Posay

PENGORSE POLDARK of TRESILVA

Ugo De Villa Sainval

INT CH Xorba De Chaponay

Quatna of Milton

Zethus De Chaponay of Tresilva

Sapajou De Villa Sainval

Veronique De Villa Sainval

Toscane De Villa Sainval

Tresilva Marianne

INT CH Xorba De Chaponay

Zethus De Chaponay of Tresilva

Veronique De Villa Sainval

Tresilva Aura

Rava Regal Valor of Reenroy

Carlisle Circe of Tresilva

Jenny Vive De Carlise

poor conformation or any other fault, known to be carried by any dog named in the pedigree, will cause the in-breeding to be a disaster, as these faults will certainly occur in puppies resulting from such a close alliance.

In-breeding has always been a source of controversy, but this method does not produce faults, as I have said. What it does do is emphasise both the good and bad genes, as these will be inherited from both parents.

It can strengthen dominants and will always reveal recessives. In-breeding is not considered to produce any degeneration but it does make obvious both the faults and virtues. This can be of value, as it will enable the breeder to recognise, and endeavour to eradicate, unwanted defects in future breeding programmes. It must be understood that in-breeding will always "fix" desired traits, as well as undesirable traits.

Before using this method a breeder must make quite sure that both the sire and dam are completely free of any defect, no matter how insignificant. In-breeding is a very potent tool but it can also be somewhat dangerous.

LINE BREEDING

This method is by far the most popular and is considered the safest and most successful of all methods of breeding. Line breeding is the mating of breeding stock with one or more common ancestors of outstanding merit. Line breeding to an animal that only appears once in a pedigree, unless it is found in the first generation, is of little worth. The more times the name of an ancestor of merit appears, the greater the chance of successful results. In line breeding, as in in-breeding, the first consideration must be the quality and excellence of any stud dog to which any bitch is to be mated.

OUT-CROSSING

This is the mating of animals which, in general, have no common ancestors. This method on the whole results in mediocre stock but can, on occasions, produce a worthwhile litter. A complete out-cross in the Bichon Frisé is more or less impossible. If any Bichon pedigree is researched back far enough, at a guess no further than ten generations at the most, the same distant ancestors will appear.

MATING AND PREGNANCY

Most bitches come into season every six months, but this can vary. Bitches have been known to have cycles varying from five months to a year, but the normal cycle is every six months.

The first sign of the bitch coming into season is the enlargement of the vaginal opening, which swells noticeably. Within the following few days there will be a bright red discharge. The discharge will gradually pale in colour, becoming less apparent. The vulva will still be swollen but it will become soft and moist. When the bitch reaches this stage, the time for mating is imminent.

THE RIGHT DAY?

Although all bitches are attractive to dogs from the onset of their season, the actual time when the bitch is willing to accept the stud dog does vary. Towards the end of the second week, on the eleventh or twelfth day, is usually considered satisfactory but this is not always successful. Some bitches are ready for mating on the fourth day, others as late as the twentieth. The red discharge has been known to continue for the whole of the bitch's season, which makes it very difficult to assess the right time for mating, but if the bitch is moving her tail invitingly from side to side this is usually an indication that she is ready to accept the stud dog.

I have also known of bitches starting to show colour again even after they have been successfully mated, but they have still produced a healthy litter.

As the instinct to reproduce in both the dog and the bitch is very strong, matings are usually satisfactory.

THE COLOURLESS SEASON

Even more difficult to assess are bitches that experience what is called a "silent season", which is a normal season without any sign of blood, often referred to as a colourless season. These bitches will produce puppies, but judging the right time for mating can be difficult.

The best way to ensure a successful mating is to watch the actions of the bitch. The only sure time is when the bitch indicates she is ready, which she will do by standing rigid with her tail to one side, even when in company of other bitches, and by the softening of the vulva.

THE MATING

A soon as the bitch comes into season you must contact the owner of the stud dog of your choice. Although bitches are normally taken to the stud dog, it is preferable if the stud can visit the bitch, especially if she is a maiden, who will be far more relaxed in familiar surroundings.

Before the mating takes place do allow the dog and bitch to play together. They should be introduced to one another while still on a lead, just in case the bitch is a little unfriendly. Once you are sure there is no sign of aggression they can be released. Many a mating is made difficult by too much interference by the owners. Natural matings are the most satisfactory. I strongly object to force-matings. After all, if the bitch refuses to allow the dog to mate her, she just is not ready for mating and to force-mate her is cruel and unnecessary. As soon as the bitch is standing quietly with her tail held to one side, she should be held gently by the collar, allowing the dog to mount her. Do not let the dog worry her unduly until she is ready. Maiden

BICHON STUD DOGS

Am. Ch. Chaminade Mr. Beau Monde: Top producing and most influential sire in American breed history with 71 Champion offspring including top winners and top producers in their own right. Bred by Barbara Stubbs, owned by Richard Beauchamp and Pauline Waterman.

Aus. Eng. Ch. Leijazulip Jazz of Zudiki. Bred by Vera Goold & Derek Chiverton, owned and exhibited by Jo Brown Emmerson. Exported to Australia.

Photo: Michael Trafford.

Eileen Beeston's Ch. Edelweiss Ebony Eyes.

Photo: Russell Fine Art.

Ch. Roushka Dance Master, bred and owned owned by Den Thomas. Photo: David Dalton.

Ch. Sibon Sloane Ranger at Pamplona. Bred by Marion Binder, owned by Michael Coad, exported to the USA.   Photo: David Dalton.

Ch. Orpheus Orion of Atroya, bred and owned by Helen Banfield.

bitches are inclined to give a sharp yap and try to pull away at the moment of penetration, so hold the bitch's collar firmly.

THE TIE
The tie is caused by a circle of muscle just inside the vulva gripping the enlarged base of the penis which will not subside until these muscles of the vulva relax. The bitch is responsible for the length of the tie, not the dog.

The actual mating is over quite quickly but the tie can be of quite a long duration. As soon as the tie occurs the dog will turn on his own, or if necessary he can be helped, by lifting one foreleg over the bitch's back so both forelegs are on the same side, then the hind leg can also be lifted, so they

Eileen Beeston's Ch. Fionavar Billy Whizzes About Asilene.

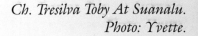

Ch. Tresilva Toby At Suanalu.
Photo: Yvette.

are standing back to back. The tie lasts for approximately 20 minutes but can take much longer. The handler will require a cushion to sit on during this period as the dog or bitch may wander about and, if allowed to do so, will drag the other dog around, so it is necessary to hold both their tails firmly together.

As soon as the dog withdraws, remove the bitch to her bed and, after a drink, she should be allowed to rest for at least half an hour.

Providing the mating was successful a second mating is not required, but if it is a maiden bitch, or there is any doubt about the mating's success, a repeat mating within forty-eight hours may be given. Most owners of stud dogs will offer a free mating when the bitch next comes into season if the mating has not produced any puppies.

The stud fee should be paid after the mating. The owner of the stud dog should give you a receipt and a signed form giving the dog's name and registration number with your national kennel club, including the date of the mating.

To reduce the risk of a high infestation of worms in the puppies it is wise to give the bitch a stool check and worm her just before the mating if necessary.

AFTER THE MATING

Once the bitch has been mated she should be treated quite normally, and for the first three weeks she will not require any extra food, but what she does eat must be of the highest quality, rich in protein, with a vitamin and mineral supplement which should be given daily.

After the fifth or sixth week, when you will be fairly sure she is in whelp, her appetite will increase. Then it is advisable to feed her twice a day.

In addition to the protein meals, food rich in calcium should be added, such as eggs, milk and cheese. Do not give too much cereal or biscuit as the bulk will make her uncomfortable; the food needs to be of high quality, not great in quantity. If, as time goes on, she appears to be heavy in whelp, three smaller meals a day will be preferable.

One of the most important necessities for the expectant mother is exercise. She should be taken for gentle walks right up to the time of whelping. Lack of exercise can often be the cause of slow and difficult whelping.

9 *WHELPING AND REARING A LITTER*

I am never quite certain that the bitch is in whelp until the sixth week after mating. It is from this time that bitches can be seen to be putting on weight. If you really need to know that she is in whelp it is always possible to have the bitch scanned. I prefer to wait and see, and it is usually possible to tell by the sixth week.

When you are sure your bitch is in whelp, extra food is essential. Also it is quite a good idea to get her accustomed to her whelping kennel. She should be encouraged to sleep in it for a short time during the day and, towards the end, to sleep in it at night. A bitch is more likely to be at ease if she is in surroundings she already knows.

EQUIPMENT

There are several items you will need for the puppies' arrival. Not all may be required but it is wise to be prepared.

The whelping kennel, or bed, must be large enough for the bitch to lie full length in it and leave enough room for the puppies to move around in it. A strong box with a front opening and a hinged lid is ideal. This box should be placed in a quiet room or corner, where the litter will be free from disturbances. As bitches are in the habit of whelping during the night, and as it is possible the bitch may whelp early, do provide a comfortable chair for yourself. Bitches should be under surveillance day and night for the last week.

To prevent the bitch carrying the puppies all around the room, the box should be surrounded with some sort of enclosure similar to a child's play-pen. Puppy-pens can be purchased from most pet shops. Always make sure the bars on the enclosure are close-set; if they are too wide the puppies may get their heads caught between the bars.

You will need several warm rough towels, which may be required for stimulating and drying the puppies, and a bowl of hot water and diluted disinfectant in which to wash your hands. Have close by a pair of fairly blunt sterilised scissors. Sterilise the scissors by boiling them in water for a few minutes. Cotton wool (cotton), Vaseline, a spool of cotton thread which may be needed to tie the umbilical cord, and a thermometer are all essential items.

A hot-water bottle should be placed in a small basket or a box, covered with a blanket. When another puppy is about to be born this basket is a useful place in which to put the other whelps while the mother is busy with the new arrival.

As new-born puppies require a high temperature of between 75 and 80 degrees F, (23.9 C – 26.7 degrees C) an infra-red lamp or a heated pad is essential. You will need at least three pieces of synthetic fleece. These absorb moisture and are easy to wash. Plenty of newspaper to scatter on the floor will be necessary. This is especially needed when the puppies are about three weeks old. When they start to move around, they will very quickly get accustomed to using the paper whenever nature calls.

PARTURITION

Whelping normally occurs on the 62nd day after mating. Bitches have been known to whelp as early as the 57th day, while others can be as late as the 65th day. If nothing has happened after that day, then it is wise to consult your vet.

It is usually about 24 hours before the onset of labour that the bitch becomes very restless. She will twist and turn, spending hours endeavouring to make a nest by scratching up masses of the newspaper which you have placed in the whelping box, panting and giving the appearance of producing a puppy very soon. Then, much to your surprise, after this activity she will go soundly to sleep, often for quite a long period of time!

TEMPERATURE

If her temperature is taken at this time and has fallen below the normal 101.4F (39.5C) she will go into labour within 24 hours. The restless and scratching stage can go on for several days. By checking the temperature every day the breeder can relax until it has dropped by two degrees. It is normal for the bitch to refuse any food when labour is imminent.

LABOUR

There are very few signs of the commencement of labour but as time goes on the contractions can be seen as ripples running down the bitch's body. These contractions are, at first, far apart, but as time goes by they will occur at closer intervals. Soon the water bag will appear, which looks rather similar to a small brown balloon. This will burst and shortly afterwards, within the hour, the first puppy should appear.

If labour pains continue for more than two hours without anything happening, or they appear to be getting weaker, or a puppy has not appeared within an hour of the water bag bursting, or if the bitch is restless and has been straining for some time without a puppy appearing, call your vet.

After the arrival of the first puppy the rest of the litter will follow at varying intervals. Sometimes the puppies arrive in quick succession, or there may be long intervals between the births – several hours is not unknown. Between the arrival of puppies your bitch may appreciate a drink of glucose mixed in milk or water.

Do not worry if Bichon puppies are born feet first; only in the large-headed breeds can such a birth be difficult.

It is not unusual for maiden bitches to be somewhat confused when the first puppy is born. If she seems at a loss and does not bite open the sac surrounding the puppy, you must release the puppy at once. Open the sac with your fingers so that the whelp can breathe. Any fluid around the mouth must be wiped clean.

Next you must cut the cord. Squeeze the cord approximately half-way along its length, pushing any blood towards the puppy's body. Use the cotton thread and tie it tightly around the cord, then cut the cord on the side away from the puppy with the sterile scissors.

Rub the puppy vigorously until it cries, at which point, usually, instinct will now prompt the bitch and she will then take care of the puppy.

Any signs of agitation on the part of the owner will disturb the whelping bitch, so talk to the bitch gently and try to stay cool and calm, just keeping a wary eye in case things go wrong.

I would like to emphasise that whelping is a completely natural process. The bitch should be allowed to produce her litter without too much interference. It is only when the whelping appears to be abnormal that any assistance is needed. Even a bitch producing her first litter will, by instinct, know the right way to open the sac, break the umbilical cord and wash the new-born puppy. She will normally, if permitted, also eat the afterbirth. Some breeders remove the afterbirth, as they consider it upsets the bitch's stomach. I let bitches eat one or two as I consider this helps to replenish minerals and nutriments. Always check that the afterbirth has been expelled after each puppy is born.

As there is always a lot of discharge when the puppies arrive, the bitch's rear end does look a sorry sight, but for the first two days do not attempt to clean her up, just do what you can without removing her from the nest and without using any water. That could make her coat and tail damp, which cannot be good for the puppies.

I always make a note of the time of birth and, if it does not upset the bitch too much, I weigh each puppy as soon as possible after birth.

It is wise to ask your vet to examine both the dam and the puppies as soon after the whelping as possible, just to make sure all are quite fit and healthy.

WARMTH

The most important vital necessity for the new-born puppy, in addition to its food, is warmth. Although the suckling reflex is very strong at birth, if the puppies are cold this reflex will become weak.

Unless the weather is really hot puppies can get cold even when snuggled up to their mother. This is because puppies at birth have a much lower body temperature than the adult Bichon. Their temperature for the first days can be as low as between 94F (34.4C) and 99F (37.2C) which is quite usual. Therefore, as the shivering reflex which helps to keep it warm does not develop until the puppy is eight days old, it is vital the puppies are kept very warm. A temperature between 75F (23.9C) and 80F (26.7C) is required, especially for the first week.

Extra heat can be provided by an infra-red lamp which must be securely hung over the whelping box, or a heated pad placed under the bedding. I personally prefer the lamp, as it is easier to control.

You may think that this extra heat may be too much for the bitch, but providing she can move a few inches away from the direct heat while still being in close contact with her puppies and is given a constant supply of fresh water, she will be quite content.

SUPPLEMENT FEEDING

If for any reason the bitch is unable to feed her puppies, or she has produced a large litter, to ensure the puppies' survival it may be necessary to supplement their food yourself. For this task a premature puppy feeder is essential. This can be a premature baby bottle and teat, available from high-class pharmacists, or a small feeder sold at pet shops for puppies. All feeding utensils must be kept scrupulously clean and sterilised.

If the bitch cannot feed the puppies they must be fed every two hours day and night. Sit with your legs crossed and covered with a rough towel. Place the puppy's rear legs on the lower knee with the body sloping upwards and the front legs resting on your upper leg. Gently open the puppy's mouth and insert the teat. In this position the puppy will be able to knead the towel as it suckles.

There is another method used to feed new-born puppies, which is by a tube. Personally I do not like or recommend this method on Bichons, as it can be quite dangerous.

There are foods made especially for the needs of premature and very young puppies which, when fed strictly according to the directions on the tin or packet, are invaluable. It is a wise precaution to have a small stock of premature puppy food just in case it is needed.

Glucose, if mixed with either milk or

water, provides a sustaining drink for the bitch both during and after labour.

Orphan puppies are a more difficult problem. If possible, try to find a foster mother. Your vet may be able to help, as he may know of a bitch who has recently whelped. This is by far the best solution; otherwise the puppies must be fed as above, with the added necessity of having to stimulate each puppy to defecate and urinate by gently stroking the anal and genital areas with slightly damp cotton-wool (cotton).

HAPPY PUPPIES

If the puppies are happy and contented they will be quite quiet; any crying is a sign that the puppy is either hungry or cold. Constant crying when well fed and warm with the mother in the nest is a sign that all is not well. It could be that the mother's milk is too acid for the pups but I strongly advise that you call for your vet immediately.

The average weight at birth varies between five and seven ounces; puppies weighing less than five ounces need constant attention as they may require supplementary feeding. Also, if the puppies vary in weight, you must keep an eye on the smaller ones as they may find it difficult to feed because the larger siblings are inclined to push the little ones off the teats. If any of the puppies do not appear to be gaining weight satisfactorily, a daily supplementary feed will be necessary until they are strong enough to fend for themselves.

A Bichon puppy pictured soon after birth.

The main concerns are eating and sleeping

One week old – the eyes and ears are both closed.

114

THE EARLY DAYS

All puppies lose a little weight when first born; however, they should double their weight by the end of the first week. The best way to be sure all are gaining weight is to weigh them at birth and once a day for the first two weeks. This is important, as this is the only way I know to ensure all are thriving. Use your kitchen scales covered with a small blanket.

Between one and three weeks puppies, when sleeping, can be seen to twitch; this reflex will disappear by three weeks. A puppy can stand by three weeks and it will walk and run by four weeks.

Eyes open between 10 and 16 days, and at this time the eyes must be protected from bright lights. The ears open at approximately thirteen days. By four weeks the puppies will recognise their owners. The 28 milk teeth will also start to erupt at four weeks.

Once the puppies' eyes are fully open and they are moving around, get them used to your voice and to being gently handled.

Providing the puppies are all thriving, the dewclaws should be removed 48 hours after birth. Remove the bitch to another room or into the garden while this task is carried out.

As the claws on young puppies grow quite quickly, becoming needle sharp, these must be kept short, otherwise they cause much discomfort to the bitch when they are feeding.

For the first three weeks of their lives the dam will both feed and clean her puppies. Nevertheless do check that they are scrupulously clean, and their box must be kept clean, both in and around their bed.

While the bitch continues to feed her puppies she must have plenty of nutritious food, at least three meals with plenty of protein and a spot of cod-liver oil a day. Add a spoonful of glucose to her water bowl, which must always be kept well filled.

Bichon bitches are very good mothers and they should be allowed to stay with their puppies for as long as they wish. I personally consider that it is unkind to prevent a bitch from seeing and playing with her puppies during the first six weeks of their lives.

Breeders must always be prepared for emergencies, and must understand that after whelping and while the bitch is feeding her puppies there are certain conditions which can seriously affect her health, which may occur during this time. Namely...

ECLAMPSIA

Eclampsia is caused by a sudden lack of calcium in the blood of the nursing bitch. The symptoms are a wild expression, panting, shaking, a staggering gait, restlessness and muscular rigidity, and her temperature can rise to 105F (40.5C).

The onset of eclampsia is very quick and will be fatal if not treated

By three weeks of age, the puppies have made rapid progress.

Photo: Marc Henrie.

immediately. It is essential that the assistance of your vet be sought without delay, as the bitch requires an immediate intravenous injection of calcium to save her life. If this unfortunate attack occurs the bitch can no longer feed her puppies.

It is a misconception to think that by giving a nursing bitch doses of calcium eclampsia can be prevented. Bitches do not store calcium; all they do not use is expelled.

MASTITIS
This is inflammation of the mammary glands caused by an excess of milk and is extremely painful. Your vet must be consulted immediately.

METRITIS
Once again there will be a rise in temperature, the bitch will appear lethargic, and she will lose interest in the puppies. This may be the result of a retained placenta, so consult your vet.

PUPPY CARE FROM THREE TO EIGHT WEEKS
For the first three weeks of their lives the puppies, providing the bitch is in good health, will require very little attention. The bitch will feed them and will make sure they are kept clean and warm.

As soon as their eyes are open the puppies will start to explore their surroundings. They are quite likely to climb out of their whelping box, but if they find it difficult to get back into their nest they could become frightened and cold, so do provide a small step, or a ramp laid the length of the opening, which will make it easy for the puppies to scramble in and out of the nest.

Puppies at this age, and for quite a time onwards, will chew anything, so provide a few of the toys which are sold especially for puppies when they are teething. This just might prevent damage to things of value such as shoes and furniture – but I did say 'might'!

116

Feed the puppies in separate bowls.

Photo: Marc Henrie.

If the weather is cold keep the room where the whelping box is situated very warm; it should not drop below 70F. Warmth is still important when the puppies are exploring their surroundings. Although the bitch will not want to stay constantly with her puppies as they get older, as a good mother she will never be far away. She will always pop in to feed and clean them when she hears any of them crying.

WEANING

This is one of the most important phases in a puppy's life, so it is essential that it is carried out with patience. It is equally essential that the right food is given in the right quantities. It will very much depend on the size of the litter when weaning should commence. If it is a big litter weaning should start at three weeks, otherwise four weeks is usually considered early enough.

As the puppies will still be getting an ample supply of milk from the bitch it is important that they are introduced to their new diet before allowing them to

feed from the bitch. Weaning is far less difficult when the puppies are really hungry.

Choose a time when they have just woken and before they have had the opportunity to feed from the bitch's milk. I have found, from experience, that instead of starting puppies on a milky meal it is better to try a meat meal. The quickest way to introduce them to solid food is to start by giving them a tiny piece of butcher's raw scraped beef. Roll a small portion of meat, about the size of a marble. Hold

A play-pen is an invaluable item of equipment. Photo: Marc Henrie.

By four weeks, individual personalities have started to emerge.

Photo: Marc Henrie.

this between your finger and thumb with a small portion protruding. Once the puppies smell the meat they will start to suck it at first, but once a puppy gets the taste it will usually eat the rest with relish.

Start with one meal a day for three days, then twice a day for a few more days, then at least three small meat meals a day. In addition the puppies can be given breakfast. As soon as they are used to the scraped beef, they will quickly learn to lap up a warm milk meal. This may be cow's or goat's milk mixed with a cereal, or one of the commercial brands prepared especially for young puppies.

By the tenth day they should be having three meat meals of about an ounce each meal – but the quantity will really depend on the size of the puppy – plus two milk meals, always freshly prepared.

Once the puppies are eating and drinking with ease, toasted wholemeal bread or a puppy meal can be added to both meat and milk meals. The quantities given should be increased gradually.

All puppies should be fed in separate dishes which will enable you to check that every puppy is getting its fair share. If they are fed in one dish the biggest puppy will eat more than its share and the smallest may go hungry. Quantities of food given will vary according to the weight of each puppy. Meals should always be given at regular intervals at the same time each day.

At between five and six weeks, the mother should be kept away from the puppies for progressively longer periods. This is not always possible, as some bitches insist on seeing their puppies right up to eight weeks. If this is the case, make sure the puppies have eaten before their mother returns to them.

There is one other natural instinct on the part of the mother which is often a surprise to owners. As her milk recedes the bitch will, if she is near her puppies after she has eaten, regurgitate her food for them. This will do no harm, providing she has not eaten any large lumps which may choke a puppy, but it will mean that the bitch will require another meal. This is best avoided by keeping the bitch away from her puppies for at least an hour after she has eaten her own meal.

All puppies should be examined, especially after eating, to make sure they are quite clean, as their faces will become very soiled with food, which is very unhygienic unless they are kept spotlessly clean. Once the puppies are eating other foods it is not unusual for a bitch to stop cleaning the puppies. She may still clean their faces but refuse to deal with the tail area. If this happens then this job must now be tackled by the breeder. Puppies never soil their sleeping quarters, so make sure there is plenty of paper accessible outside their sleeping area.

.

WORMING

Puppies must be treated against roundworms at four weeks and then at two-week intervals up to the age of three months. Medication should always be obtained from your vet.

SOCIALISATION

Although new-born puppies and their mother require peace and quiet for the first few weeks, by the time they are four weeks of age puppies should learn to accept loud and unusual noises. This is best achieved by allowing them to become accustomed to the daily household noises, such as the vacuum cleaner, the radio and television.

Encourage all the family and friends to pick them up to pet them and generally make a fuss of each puppy, as often as possible. This treatment will make them used to people handling them. If puppies are introduced to loud noises and various different people from a very young age they will never suffer from nerves. It is the isolated puppy, kept away from general household noise and people, who will find it difficult later when confronted with crowds.

As the puppies mature they will require more and more exercise which

The expert can now start assessing conformation. Photo: Marc Henrie.

An evenly matched litter, pictured at seven weeks.   Photo: Marc Henrie.

At eight weeks, it is time for the puppies to go to their new homes.   Photo: Marc Henrie.

they will provide for themselves by wrestling and sparring with each other. Whenever the weather permits, fresh air and a free run in the garden are essential for their wellbeing – but this must be under supervision. Puppies have no sense of danger. They do not understand heights or depths, and what is more, they think everything they find is something to eat. These are some of the reasons why you must always keep an eye on them, especially in the garden.

And I stress again that, as the Bichon's coat does not shed, a daily brushing is necessary. Even at this very young age a light comb and brush can be used with advantage; it will accustom puppies to grooming in the future.

10 HEALTH CARE AND HEREDITARY DISEASES

BY TREVOR TURNER B. Vet. Med. MRCVS FRSH

The choice of your vet is really just as important as the choice of puppy. If you have never owned a dog before, you should know that every breed, even the Bichon Frisé, has its own idiosyncrasies and you will need a veterinary surgeon with some knowledge and rapport with the breed. Remember that a person who may have a reputation for being good with cats, or super with St Bernards, may not necessarily be the ideal vet for small dogs!

CHOOSING YOUR VET
How do you set about choosing your vet? If you have, or have had, other animals, or know of a local vet by reputation, the task is much easier. Otherwise look in your classified telephone directory, which will at least make you familiar with the names and whereabouts of the local practices. Do not be afraid to approach people exercising vaguely similar dogs in your area and enquire where they go for

veterinary attention and what they think of the service. I suggest approaching people with Yorkshire Terriers, Poodles, Pugs and other small dogs rather than the owners of large dogs such as Boxers, Labradors or Rottweilers. Very often you will find that one name will crop up more frequently, and that is the practice to try first.

Even before you acquire your dog do not be afraid to phone practices and enquire about details of service. Explain that you are about to acquire a Bichon Frisé and ask them if they are likely to encounter any particular problems. The quality of the reply from the reception staff will at least give you some idea of the service you are likely to receive subsequently.

If you are not impressed, do not be afraid to try elsewhere, because the decision you are making is an important one. It is far better to choose carefully before you establish a relationship than to have to change vets at a later stage.

Trevor Turner
B.Vet.Med.
MRCVS pictured
with Jackie
Ransom.

Photo: Marc
Henrie.

Fees and premises will vary. Do not be impressed too much by either, initially; the quality of the service, availability at unsocial hours and willingness to discuss problems are probably more important.

THE FIRST VISIT

Having acquired your puppy from the breeder you will undoubtedly have received instructions about the timing of inoculations and suggestions on when you should visit a vet. This should not be delayed too long after acquiring the puppy so that the vet can check for any hereditary or congenital problems that may have inadvertently escaped the notice of the breeder. However, it is a good idea to let the puppy settle down in the new surroundings of your home for a day or two before subjecting it to yet another strange experience! The first visit is often the time for starting vaccination as well as a general health check.

GENERAL HEALTH CHECK

The vet will probably examine the puppy very thoroughly to make sure that you have bought a healthy animal. Do not resent this and please do not get upset if the puppy appears to object to part of the examination. It does not understand the reason for it and not surprisingly may object vociferously to the examination, particularly of its private parts!

When vets carry out this examination they are looking for far more than, for example, signs of enteritis or general health. They will examine the skin to make sure there is no eczema, mange or dermatitis present. This will also include a check on the ears. Bichons Frisés as a breed carry a lot of hair around, sometimes in the ear canal, and you may be shown how to remove some of this hair to keep the ear free of obstruction.

The check will include an examination of the bony skeleton. Even in a young puppy abnormalities such as slipping kneecaps can sometimes be revealed which could later lead to lameness. The eyes, nose and mouth will be checked to make sure there are no deformities. A male's testes will be checked to see if they are descended and in the scrotum.

While this examination is proceeding, the vet will probably be asking you questions about feeding and general behaviour. Do not hesitate at this stage to discuss any worries you may have, no matter how trivial you may think them.

A worming programme is also usually suggested at this time. This may be slightly different from the worming routine that has been suggested by the breeder, but do mention any instructions you have been given.

PUPPIES WITH PROBLEMS

Most Bichon Frisé puppies will pass the health examination without difficulty, but what happens if the veterinary surgeon does find a problem? It may be a physical problem and can be quite minor, for example an abnormality of the bite when the upper and lower jaws do not meet in the correct manner; or there may be joint problems that, although minor, could lead to lameness later in life. Temperament problems may sometimes cause the vet concern

and need discussion. Any of these problems may be acquired or congenital, that is, either due to injury or else present from birth.

If the puppy has severe problems the vet may suggest that the puppy is returned to the breeder. This is one of the reasons why it is worthwhile ensuring that your puppy has its first veterinary examination within a short time of you buying it. If you do not want to return the puppy, be sure to discuss this with your vet at the time. Remember he or she is working in your best interests. A vet will not be unsympathetic but has a job to do and will carefully explain to you the implications of the problem, and then the decision must rest with you.

ROUTINE HEALTH CARE

Having finished the physical examination the vet will discuss feeding, general management, training, worming and vaccination. Remember that when you take a puppy to the vet, even just for vaccination, the cost includes a consultation and that means what it says! Any worries, doubts or problems should be discussed with the vet at this time, no matter how trivial. Do not be shy about making a list of questions you want to ask. Many people feel embarrassed at taking out a list in front of the vet, but do not worry; most vets will be pleased that you have taken the trouble to make one.

If the puppy is a bitch you may want

123

to breed, now is a good time to discuss it, and the problem of heats (oestrus). And what are the alternatives to breeding? The vet will discuss surgical neutering (spaying) or chemical control of oestrus with either injections or tablets.

Many novice owners acquire a male puppy and feel they would like to show it and breed from it. This is not quite as easy as it appears at first sight, and the vet will be happy to discuss the various aspects involved.

VACCINATIONS

If the puppy is old enough and fit enough vaccination may begin on your first visit. The vaccination programme your vet recommends may well vary from that suggested by the breeder or that of friends with puppies. Vaccination programmes are tailored to the puppy and depend on the incidence of disease in the area, age, breed and other factors.

Most puppies can be vaccinated from about eight weeks old. Canine vaccines usually involve at least two injections, the second one given at around 12 weeks of age. These injections give good protection against major canine diseases, but do remember that no vaccine gives complete protection against any particular disease. However, today's vaccines give a high degree of protection for all the diseases included in the programme.

INOCULATION PROGRAMME: CANINE PARVOVIRUS

This disease is transmitted by a very resistant virus which can live away from the dog's body for long periods of time. Vaccination gives extremely good protection but it must be boosted annually. Symptoms of the disease are depression, vomiting and diarrhoea, often with blood. Treatment involves intensive care and intravenous fluid therapy and is frequently unsuccessful.

DISTEMPER

This is the virus disease which, in the 1930s, first led to canine vaccination. Although now less common than in the past it still occurs in epidemic form from time to time. The signs can include vomiting and diarrhoea but usually the animal appears to have a cold, with runny eyes and nose and often a cough. Later nervous signs can develop with twitching and even fits and paralysis.

HARDPAD

A form of distemper which causes hardening of the pads. The same vaccination gives protection against distemper and hardpad. Again a yearly booster dose is recommended.

CANINE HEPATITIS

Another virus disease against which vaccines give protection. Hepatitis is inflammation of the liver and other internal organs. It is generally referred to as canine adenovirus1 or CAV1 disease. Infection is contracted from both faeces and urine, and dogs who have recovered from the disease may act as carriers. Signs can include acute hepatitis, hence the original name, but the kidneys are much more commonly affected. The virus can also affect the lungs and cause a respiratory form of the disease but this is more commonly caused by an allied virus, CAV2, which is part of the kennel cough complex of diseases. Inoculation against CAV1 and CAV2 generally provides good protection.

LEPTOSPIROSIS

A bacterial rather than a viral disease but it is incorporated in the canine vaccination programme. Serious illness can result from infection and it can also affect humans. There are two forms in the dog, of which *Leptospira icterohaemorrhagiae* can be passed to humans.

The symptoms include fever, jaundice and severe depression. The other form in the dog, *Leptospira canicola*, is also called lamp-post disease since it is transmitted by dogs sniffing at one another's urine. The signs are acute kidney problems.

Unlike virus diseases leptospiral diseases can be treated with antibiotics, but prevention is better than cure. Again an annual booster is essential for continuing protection.

INFECTIOUS RHINOTRACHEITIS

The so-called cough syndrome, is popularly known as kennel cough, although it can affect animals that have never been near kennels. It is a highly infectious condition and is caused by a mixture of virus and bacteria. Again, vaccination provides protection. In addition an intranasal vaccine is widely available which covers the most important bacterial component of the disease, *Bordatella bronchiseptica*. This vaccine is particularly useful if there is an outbreak of cough in your area or you are about to board your dog. So ask your vet's advice. Bear in mind, however, that this vaccine only provides protection for about six months.

RABIES

With the current strict quarantine laws the UK is rabies-free and rabies vaccination is not usually carried out unless the animal is intended for export. In many countries of the world puppies need their rabies shots at about the same time as their other inoculations.

AILMENTS AND DISEASES

Bichons Frisés, although a small breed, are anything but delicate. They are healthy, hardy little dogs. They have few problems specific to the breed but they do suffer doggy ailments, the most important of which are described below.

ANAL PROBLEMS

Both dogs and bitches have two small scent glands on either side of the anus. These are normally emptied when the dog defecates. Sometimes, however, things go wrong and they can fill up and cause problems. Signs can vary, but excessive licking underneath, biting the tail head, or sometimes scooting or dragging the bottom along the ground are warning signals.

Anal sac problems can sometimes be caused by worms, diarrhoea or infection, and a visit to the vet is a reasonable precaution. Usually, though, it is just a simple impaction of the glands, in which case the vet may show you how to empty them yourself. Once trouble has started some Bichons Frisés develop a fixation about their anal glands and often bite or chew in the groin or at the base of the tail, particularly when they are under stress. In these cases, if persistent, the vet may advise surgical removal of the glands to provide a permanent solution to the problem and give the pet some peace.

Sometimes, especially in puppies or dogs whose coats have become very overgrown, problems due to faecal mats will be mistaken for anal gland problems. Remember that the Standard of the Bichon Frisé states that the coat should fall in soft corkscrew curls. Occasionally, if there are too many of these around the anus, they get matted with bits of faeces, which causes soreness and discomfort, not to mention smell. Careful hygiene is really all that is necessary to prevent or cure this, at the same time ensuring that the hair length, particularly in the adult, does not become excessive around that area.

BOWEL PROBLEMS

Enteritis is every owner's dread, particularly with a puppy, but this is not the only bowel problem.

AN UPSET BOWEL

This is one of the most common ailments in dogs, and the Bichon Frisé is no exception. The most obvious sign of any bowel upset is vomiting and/or diarrhoea. Puppies eat all manner of foreign materials and assault their bowels with foreign bodies such as pebbles, bits of plastic toys etc., which can actually cause a stoppage. Other causes can be infection, poison, parasites, and allergies. A radical change of diet or too many treats can also upset the bowel's functioning.

First aid for a general bowel upset is relatively simple. Restrict, but do not prevent, fluid intake, since if a dog drinks too much it will bring it back up (and often more besides). At the same time, starve the animal for 24 hours and then offer small quantities of light, easily digested food such as fish, eggs, chicken, veal or rabbit. If there is no improvement the dog should be taken to the vet. If a dog vomits or passes blood the vet should be contacted without delay. An accompanying sample of the faeces is often an aid to the diagnosis, especially in the case of puppies.

WIND, FLATUS, OR COLIC

This is another bowel condition that can affect both the young puppy and, not uncommonly, the elderly dog. Puppies at around weaning age will often overeat and become distressed with wind. A good first-aid measure is to administer a dose of babies' gripe water or, alternatively, a preparation containing charcoal. If the puppy is very distressed a visit to the vet is essential.

In the elderly dog the problem is due to the inability of its bowel to contract in a normal manner and so after a meal the poor dog blows up with wind. Again gripe water or a charcoal preparation are good first-aid measures. Changing your dog's feeding regime to include more frequent, smaller meals will also do a lot to help. If the condition is severe and the dog in pain, obviously the vet should be contracted.

HAEMORRHAGIC ENTERITIS

In many small breeds simple inflammation of the bowel (enteritis), vomiting and diarrhoea can quickly progress to the haemorrhagic where the poor animal is passing blood at both ends. Canine parvovirus is often the cause of this in puppies but other causes, including toxaemia, shock and infection, can be responsible in adult dogs. This condition is dangerous and your vet should be contacted without delay. The animal usually wants to drink copiously but do not allow this because it will only make the condition worse with the dog wanting to vomit more frequently. Ice to lick can sometimes help but it is better to give nothing by mouth and to arrange to take the patient to the vet as soon as possible.

BREATHING PROBLEMS

Bichons Frisés are relatively free from breathing problems. However, many have particularly small airways. Any infection resulting in enlargement of the tonsils can cause some respiratory distress. The signs are snorting, coughing, and respiratory distress. If this occurs a visit to the vet is necessary since a course of antibiotics is usually needed.

DENTAL PROBLEMS

DOUBLE DENTITION

This is a common problem in many of the miniature breeds but Bichons Frisés appear to suffer less than other such breeds from this condition. The deciduous, or baby, teeth are not shed when the permanent teeth are fully erupted at about six to nine months old and the dog has a double row of teeth between which food can become lodged and cause infection. If you think your dog has more teeth than it should, consult your vet.

127

TARTAR AND GUM RECESSION

Calculus and periodontal disease, to give them their correct titles, are not uncommon in the Bichon Frisé. The cause is very similar to that in humans. Invisible bacterial plaque is laid down on the teeth resulting in the deposition of tartar, which will cause the gum to recede (periodontal disease) with ultimate loosening of the teeth as the sockets become infected. Today there are specially designed toothbrushes and malt-flavoured toothpaste which are worth trying. If you can brush your dog's teeth regularly, it will help prevent tooth loss as well as ensuring that your dog has much sweeter breath and is nice to be near!

In addition regular scaling and polishing will help to preserve your dog's teeth. A dog has to have a general anaesthetic for this to be carried out efficiently.

EAR PROBLEMS

The Breed Standard states that the Bichon Frisé's ears should hang close to the head and be well covered with flowing hair. This conformation can lead to lack of ventilation, and regular maintenance in the form of grooming and plucking excess hair from the ear canal is necessary. The lack of ventilation can result in infection in the ear canal, the signs of which are often a small brown smelly discharge. If these signs are neglected the condition progresses to soreness of the ear canal and the dog may scratch and cause the whole area to become red and inflamed.

EAR MITES

These can and do occur, particularly when the Bichon Frisé shares a home with cats who carry these tiny mites, often without showing any signs of them. In the dog they can cause intense irritation: scratching and rubbing in turn lead to an inflamed ear canal, excess wax and very soon an infected ear. There are many preparations available from your vet to clear the trouble. Remember that the neglected ears can lead to chronic otitis (canker), the cure for which in many cases is fairly extensive and expensive surgery.

EYE PROBLEMS

The eyes of the Bichon Frisé should be relatively trouble-free from the point of view of conformation – their shape and set. However, the abundance of hair on their faces can lead to irritation of the eyeball and result in chronic conjunctivitis and overflow of tears (epiphora) which in turn causes tear staining on the face. This is always a problem in a white or light-coloured animal. The wetness causes irritation which in turn leads to rubbing and excoriation or ulceration of the face. The condition therefore merits constant attention. Reducing the irritation by trimming the hair does much to resolve the problem.

In some cases the tear ducts may be blocked which results in the tear overflow. In this case seek your vet's help. Treatment for the actual staining of the hair can be difficult. Pet shops stock a multiplicity of remedies, the majority of which are ineffective. If conjunctivitis and infection are both present the tear staining will be worse. In this case antibiotics, sometimes taken over a long period, will improve matters. In any case discuss the matter with your vet before trying any of the over-the-counter remedies.

FITS AND COLLAPSE
A dog in a fit is unconscious and not aware of what is happening. Onlookers certainly are – and very frightening it can be. Fits occur for many reasons and generally last only a few seconds, during which a dog may urinate and defecate. When the dog comes out of the fit it can neither see nor hear properly for a short while and it may even bite its owner in self-defence.

Fits in puppies can be due to infections such as distemper, as well as worms, colic and many other causes. Collapse is very uncommon in the Bichon Frisé but can occur in the older dog due to defective circulation or heart problems.

HEART DISEASES
These are relatively infrequent in the breed except in the older obese animal, when the first sign is often a chronic cough, particularly when the dog becomes excited, and first gets up from rest.

HIP PROBLEMS
Many of the Toys and other small breeds suffer from problems involving the hip joint. Legg-Perthes disease, an enlargement and degeneration of the head of the femur, occurs at around five months of age just before the puppy is full-grown and is due to failure of the blood supply to the hip during the growth period. Corrective surgery is usually extremely successful. Hip dysplasia is not considered to be a problem to which Bichons are prone.

LAMENESS
Slipping kneecaps, slipping stifle, or, more correctly, luxation of the patellae, is not unknown in the Bichon Frisé and often results in the intermittent lifting of one or both hindlegs when walking or running. It can be due to an injury such as a strain, but is more likely to be of congenital origin. Although any hereditary implications have not been fully worked out it is obviously sensible not to breed from affected animals. With modern veterinary orthopaedic surgery correction of the condition even in very young animals can be remarkably successful.

OBESITY
Overweight should not be a problem if your dog is correctly fed and not over-

129

indulged. However, many middle-aged Bichons Frisés do seem to become overweight. This is usually due to over-indulgence with the wrong foods. Do take your vet's advice and do not be afraid of consulting him or her if you think your dog is getting a little plump. Bichons Frisés do have a long coat and this often disguises increasing girth. A weight check is the most sensible way of keeping tabs on obesity. Weigh yourself on the bathroom scales and then weigh yourself plus dog. Do this regularly, perhaps monthly, so any increase in the dog's weight will be apparent and appropriate action can be taken.

Remember that obesity can lead to breathing problems and heart disease but probably more commonly to joint problems and lameness. As a first-aid, reduce all treats especially starchy and fatty foods.

SKIN PROBLEMS
Bichons Frisés, like other white dogs, can frequently have sensitive skins. Much can be done to prevent a chronic condition developing.

ALLERGIC SKIN CONDITIONS
Contact allergies can develop due to sensitivity to plants, carpets, man-made car seat covers and other materials and objects with which your dog may come in contact. The irritation is usually on the less hairy parts of the skin, the feet and underparts and will frequently need sustained treatment to effect a cure.

ATOPY
This is an inhalation allergy, rather like hayfever and asthma in humans. In the dog, inhaled pollens can cause itching round the face and feet and other parts of the skin. Allergies caused by particular foods can occur, but these are rare.

All these allergic skin problems need veterinary help. The results can be localised or generalised eczema (dermatitis or inflammation of the skin) which causes the dog great discomfort. Although local application of antihistamine creams and lotions containing calamine will bring temporary relief the underlying cause will need to be determined.

PARASITIC SKIN PROBLEMS
Fleas and lice can also cause irritation and result in patches of eczema. Puppies should be regularly checked for fleas and lice and one of the various effective sprays or baths obtainable from your vet used regularly. Remember that fleas, unlike lice, breed away from the body and therefore the environment also has to be treated. Again your vet will recommend the appropriate products.

MANGE
This is not a great problem in the breed, unlike some other toy breeds, but it can occur. There are two forms, both due to tiny mites that burrow in the layers of the skin. Sarcoptic mange can cause scabies in humans and causes intense

irritation both in the dog and in the infected owner. Demodectic mange sometimes results in hairless patches without very much irritation and is due to a mite that lives deep in the hair follicles.

Diagnosis of either form of mange depends on skin scrapings and once diagnosed the condition can be treated accordingly. Early consultation with your vet is essential in the case of any skin problem

TRAVEL SICKNESS

Puppies and dogs of many breeds, not least among them the Bichon Frisé, can suffer from travel or motion sickness and vets are frequently consulted about this problem. Many cases can be overcome by careful training.

You should start the puppy travelling young, holding it and distracting its attention from the vehicle movement, ensuring you are well supplied with towels and covering your clothes with a plastic sheet or apron. This may do the trick! Ensure the journeys are very short. Alternatively, transport the puppy in a cardboard box so that it cannot see out through the windows and be upset by passing objects and the sensation of movement. Gradually increase the length of the journeys.

If you are not successful, try one of the many human travel sickness remedies. Most Bichon Frisé puppies require about half a tablet. There are various makes on the market available without

prescription. Different formulations are available and before consulting the vet it may be worthwhile trying different brands to see if one is effective. If you have to depend on tablets prescribed by the vet you will always have to ensure that you have them with in adequate supply.

WORMS

ROUNDWORMS

These can be particularly bothersome in puppies. They can be infested from their mothers before they are born and be passing worm eggs out in their faeces by the time they are 11 days old. Frequently evidence of the worms themselves is not apparent unless the puppy is ill and vomits. However, your vet can detect their presence by a simple faecal test and may request a sample of the puppy's stool. In any case, puppies should be regularly wormed every four weeks until they are about six months old, particularly for roundworms, although occasionally tapeworms will affect the young animal.

From six months onwards, worming with a preparation that covers roundworm, tapeworm and the other types of worm makes good sense; your vet will advise you. Today there are very safe and very effective remedies on the market which involve no inconvenience to the animal, but it is worth seeking veterinary advice before buying any remedies over the counter.

TAPEWORMS

Unlike roundworms, cannot be passed directly from dog to dog but must pass through an intermediate host. The most common urban tapeworm, *Dipylidium caninum*, has the flea as an intermediate host. In country areas, where there are more animal varieties of than in a town, a dog can be infested with different types of tapeworm. Regular deworming removes any danger to the dog.

HEARTWORM

This is a parasite that lives in the heart (actually inside the right-hand chamber of the heart) and in the major artery to the lungs. Heartworms can cause significant problems in the dog, the symptoms being easily confused with other heart diseases. Heartworm tends to be found in specific areas, usually where mosquitoes (the intermediate host) are found. Modern wormers are very effective and should be used routinely in areas where heartworm is endemic.

PET HEALTH INSURANCE

Several excellent pet health insurance schemes are available today, particularly those from specialist companies. These policies, although not covering routine vaccination, worming, whelping and dental treatment, certainly cover all unexpected veterinary bills as well as chronic conditions up to the insured limit for any one condition.

Veterinary expertise is rapidly expanding and conditions that were untreatable a few years ago are now regularly and routinely treated. Cancer is only one example of this. The expertise and care necessary for effecting these cures has to be paid for and unfortunately veterinary fees are increasing.

Talk to your vet about pet health insurance.

11

THE BICHON FRISE IN THE USA

BY BARBARA STUBBS

In May of 1973 the Bichon Frisé made its first appearance in the American show ring as a breed fully recognized by the American Kennel Club. This was a surprising accomplishment, as the breed's documented arrival in the United States did not occur until 1956 when Hélène and Francis Picault arrived in Wisconsin with three de Steren Vor Bichons from France.

LAUNCH OF THE BICHON FRISE

In 1958 the Picaults met Azalea Gascoigne, who was involved in purebred dogs with Dachshunds, and who became actively interested in this new breed. She travelled to France and returned with foundation dogs that included Lady de Frimoussettes, whose son, Dapper Dan de Gascoigne would have enormous influence in the early years.

The Picaults moved to San Diego, California where they met Gertrude Fournier, then involved with Collies carrying her Cali-col prefix. The Picaults' interest in Bichons faded and in 1963 Mrs Fournier became sole owner of their dogs. At this juncture Mayree Butler, Reenroy, acquired her first Bichon, became deeply interested in the breed and joined Mrs Fournier in her efforts to promote the Bichon Frisé. The two ladies contacted Mrs Gascoigne and in 1964 a meeting was held in San Diego. A national 'parent' club was organized, The Bichon Frisé Club of America, Inc. Official registration of the breed began and the Bichon was on its way.

DEVELOPMENT OF BREED TYPE

Through the diligent efforts of many of the early breeders and the media assistance of Richard Beauchamp, owner-editor of *Kennel Review* magazine, interest in the Bichon Frisé grew substantially. Overall quality improved with the increased participation of those who had been previously active in purebred dogs. As breed type gained greater consistency, the grooming and presentation developed to a degree that was acceptable for competition in the US show ring at that time. The style would be refined significantly through the years in the United States and would be adapted and modified according to the dictates of other countries interested in the breed.

In September of 1968 a basic Breed Standard was adopted by the Bichon Frisé Club of America as a major step toward the goal of breed recognition by the American Kennel Club. In the decade that followed it was apparent this Standard was too simplistic. Judges complained it was vague and was thus open to excessively wide degrees of interpretation. Therefore, in December of 1979 the Bichon Frisé Club of America again voted on a Standard, this time one of a more detailed nature.

In the mid-1980s the American Kennel Club began a broad programme to unify the format of all the Breed Standards. The Bichon Frisé Club of America complied with this request. Some modifications and additions were made, the requested format was used and in October of 1988 the Breed Standard in use today was adopted by the required two-thirds vote of the total parent club membership.

AKC ACCEPTANCE

In 1971 the American Kennel Club granted the Bichon Frisé acceptance into the Miscellaneous class. This gave the breed its first opportunity to be seen at AKC-sanctioned events. It offered additional exposure to the Bichon for other purebred dog fanciers who became interested, brought their expertise with them and joined the ranks of Bichon devotees.

Eighteen months later, in May of 1973, Bichons were given full breed recognition in the Non Sporting Group. This allowed competition for Championship points on the breed level plus all-breed Group and Best in Show participation. The first Group placement, a Group 2, was won on that first exciting weekend by Mrs Fournier's Cali-Col's Scalawag who would later become Am. Mex. Ch. Cali-Col's Scalawag CD. The first all-breed Best in Show would be won six weeks later by Ch. Chaminade Syncopation. The breed was on its way to unprecedented success in the United States.

FOUNDATION LINES

Mrs Fournier, Cali-Col, and Mrs Butler, Reenroy, were the foremost breeders during these early years. Outstanding dogs from these bloodlines, such as the top producers Cali-Col's Shadrack and Reenroy's Riot Act, would provide foundation dogs for many of the early breeders.

There is seldom a multi-generation

Dapper Dan de Gascoigne 1964-1977: One of the most influential sires of the early American Bichons.
Bred by Azalea Gascoigne, owned by Mayree Butler (Reenroy).

making their kennel names known throughout the Bichon world.

Jean Rank, Rank, of Pennsylvania, was another early breeder who used foundation dogs from both Reenroy and Cali-Col lines. She, in her turn, provided foundation stock for newer breeders that became involved after breed recognition in the early 1970s. The 1981 National Specialty was won by Ch. Rank's Raggedy Andy bred by Jean Rank and Judy Thayer. In addition Ch. Rank's Eddie, owned by Robert Koeppel of New York, was the first Bichon to win Best of Breed at the prestigious Westminster Kennel Club show in New York City – one of those special moments in our breed history. Robert Koeppel campaigned several breeds through the years but the Bichons were his first and favourite, and dogs from his Caralandra line were in evidence for nearly three decades.

pedigree that does not contain one or both of these influential lines. In addition to their success as breeders, both ladies were active on the national and local breed club level. This was important, as the unity and successful organization of the Bichon clubs around the country were instrumental factors in receiving AKC recognition in record-breaking time.

Mrs Fournier and Mrs Butler retired from active breeding many years ago but not before breeding forty-five and forty-four Champions respectively and

THE CALIFORNIA INFLUENCE

Dapper Dan de Gascoigne came to Southern California where he was a dominant stud dog in the breeding programmes of both Mrs Fournier and Mrs Butler. Dan was the sire of both Ch. Cali-Col's Robspierre and Ch. Reenroy's Ami du Kilkanny. In the late 1960s they were acquired by Barbara Stubbs, Chaminade, along with a second male, Petit Galant de St George. These three Bichons would have an impact that could not have been foreseen, while Barbara Stubbs would become involved in the Bichon Frisé to a degree she did not anticipate.

Robspierre and Ami were bred. In the resulting litter was Ch. Chaminade Mr Beau Monde, a dog of enormous influence. His sister, Ch. Chaminade Sonata, was bred to Petit Galant. This produced the first Best-in-Show Bichon, Ch. Chaminade Syncopation, owned by Phyllis Tabler, a noted Cocker breeder and exhibitor from New York. In addition to being the top Bichon for 1973, 1974 and 1975, Syncopation sired fourteen Champion offspring, and

his jubilant showmanship and friendly attitude won over a bevy of new fans for the breed. Petit Galant and Ami produced a son, Ch. Chaminade Tempo, who would make an impact in the 1980s.

Richard Beauchamp, of Beau Monde, acquired Ch. Chaminade Mr Beau Monde in 1971. He is the acknowledged top producing sire, with sixty-six Champions. Mr Beau Monde's offspring became top winners and producers in their own right on both the breed and all-breed levels. It was an

The Chaminade Trio: Am. Ch. Cali-Col's Robspierre, Am. Ch. Reenroy's Ami du Kilkanny and Petit Galant de St George. Foundation dogs of the Chaminade line (Barbara Stubbs). Photo: 1969.

Am. Ch. Chaminade Syncopation: The first Best in Show Bichon, top Bichon for 1973-1975-1975. Bred by Barbara Stubbs and Richard Beauchamp. Owned by Phyllis Tabler. Always shown by Ted Young.

incredible stroke of good fortune for the world of Bichons to have a dog of such dominance under the supervision of an individual with over thirty years experience of breeding and showing purebred dogs – a classic case of the right dog with the right person at the right time.

Richard Beauchamp's interest in and dedication to the Bichon Frisé has been a major factor in the success of the breed in the United States and, ultimately, in several other countries. Beauchamp and Pauline Waterman were joined in partnership from 1973 to 1986 under the Beau Monde prefix. They were the breeders of Ch. Beau

Monde the Huckster, who is fourth on the list of top producing sires with thirty-five Champions. He was one of many on a long list of well-known Bichons.

Pauline Waterman continued her breeding programme under the Joline prefix. Richard Beauchamp joined Gene and Mary Ellen Mills, Drewlaine, for continued success on both the domestic and international level. Both Mr Beauchamp and Mr Mills are AKC judges now and no longer active breeders. Mr Beauchamp has judged a great number of breeds around the world so he has become a familiar figure to exhibitors everywhere.

THE MIDDLE WEST
In the Middle West (Illinois) Dolores and Charles Wolske, C & D Bichons, would become the all-time top US Bichon breeders with an amazing one hundred and thirty-eight Champions at the time of writing! In 1972 they acquired their first Bichons, the litter-mates, Ch. C & D's Countess Becky and Ch. C & D's Count Kristopher. Becky is the number two top producing bitch of all time with sixteen Champions. This includes thirteen by Mr Beau Monde.

The 'Sun' and the 'Moon' litters were noted for producing foundation dogs for newer breeders, plus the first Best in Show Bichon bitch, Ch. C & D's Beau Monde Sunbeam. Sunbeam was owned by GeorgeAnn Slocum who had also owned the top Bichon in 1975, Ch. Keystone Christine (another Mr Beau Monde daughter). Count Kristopher produced twenty-nine Champions including the top dog of 1976, a multiple Best in Show winner, Ch. C & D's Beau Monde Blizzard. Bred to Sunbeam, Count Kristopher produced a daughter, Ch. C & D's Beau Monde The Firecracker, who is the top producing bitch of all time.

Everyone agrees that these litter-mates proved to be an absolutely amazing duo. A grandson, Ch. C & D's Xmas Knight, not only produced fourteen Champions but was an owner-handled Best in Show dog for C & D Bichons. The C & D line has provided foundation dogs for breeders for nearly three decades and has sent several Bichons abroad to provide the foundation for foreign breeding programmes.

Rosmarie Blood, Crockerly, of California was one of those who initiated their Bichon involvement with a Mr. Beau Monde-Countess Becky daughter, Ch. C & D's Beau Monde Moonshine. Moonshine produced nine Champions, six of whom were Group winners. Most notable was Ch. Crockerly Beau Monde Eclipse, owned by Nancy Shapland, who was the National Sweepstakes winner in 1979. In 1980 she was Best of Breed at the National Specialty show and No 1 Bichon for the year. Mrs Blood is now a judge and has the Non Sporting Group

and the Working Group. She has judged on many occasions in the UK and also in Australia and New Zealand.

THE EAST COAST

On the East Coast, in Virginia, John, Mary and Kathie Vogel, Vogelflight, had become interested in Bichons in the early 1970s after their involvement with other breeds. Their bitch Ch. Vogelflight's Diandee Ami Pouf was bred to Mr Beau Monde. In February of 1975 a litter of four males was born

Am. Ch. Beau Monde The Firecracker: Top producing bitch of all time with 17 Champion offspring. Bred by Richard Beauchamp and Pauline Waterman. Owned by Sherry Fry.

Am. Ch. Vogelflight's Music Man: No 1 Bichon 1976-77-78, three-time National Specialty Show winner, a top producer, second only to his father, Mr. Beau Monde. Bred by Mary Vogel, shown by Joe Waterman.

that made history. Ch. Vogelflight's Music Man won three consecutive National Specialty Shows, 1976, 1977 and 1978. The National Specialty Show is the epitome of breed competition. 'Banjo' was also the top-winning Bichon on the all-breed level for 1977 and 1978 and is second only to his sire, Mr Beau Monde, as a top producer, with forty-seven Champion offspring.

A second son, Ch. Vogelflight's Choirmaster, was a multiple Best in Show winner and No 1 Bichon for 1979. The third son, Ch. Vogelflight's Choir Boy, completed his US Championship and then went to England to the Leander Kennels of John and Wendy Streatfield. Ch. Vogelflight's Linus Diandee was the final Champion and another successful producer. The Vogels continue to breed outstanding Bichons of an easily recognized breed type – always superior movement, excellent coats and gorgeous faces. Their contribution has been consistent quality with outstanding presentation.

Another to be influenced by the C & D Bichons was Nancy Shapland, Devon, of Illinois. Her first Bichon was Ch. C & D's Star Gazer (sired by Ch. C & D Sunburst from the famous 'Sun' litter), a multiple Group winner plus that always electrifying Best of Breed win at Westminster Kennel Club, New York 1976. Next Mrs Shapland campaigned Ch. Beau Monde the Huckster, the top producer mentioned earlier, who would sire her next show dog and National Specialty winner, Ch. Crockerly Beau Monde Eclipse.

Ch. C & D's Devon Hell's Lil' Angel

Am. Ch. C and D's Xmas Knight: One of the many outstanding Champions of C and D kennels of Charles and Dolores Wolske, and the first to be owner-handled to a Best in Show.

(from the final Mr Beau Monde and Becky litter) produced five Champions for Mrs Shapland but there would be none to equal the illustrious Ch. Devon Puff and Stuff, the 'stuff' of which dreams are made. Puff was the No 1 Bichon of all time until August of 1998 when her record was finally broken. She won sixty Best in Shows, and a hundred and sixty-five Group Firsts. She won back-to-back Bichon Frisé Club of America National Specialties, 1985 and 1986, and was the top Bichon and the top Non Sporting dog during those years. Puff was also the first Bichon to win the Group at Westminster Kennel Club, a feat she accomplished in two consecutive years. In 1986 she was the No 2 dog of all breeds. Her showmanship was phenomenal and her exuberance brought joy to spectators, judges and exhibitors alike. Puff was indeed special. Mrs Shapland is now a judge of the Toy and Non Sporting breeds.

Sharan Fry, Kobold, was one of the first successful breeders in Texas. She was the owner of Ch. Beau Monde the Firecracker, the top producing dam of all time with seventeen Champions. The Kobold Bichons have had continued success for well over two decades, as the sixty-seven Champions would indicate.

THE NEXT GENERATION
In the early 1970s the Norvic line of Alice and Norman Vicha of Ohio began with a foundation bitch of solid Reenroy breeding. From their fifty-five Champions there were many standouts but none with more 'pizazz' than the multiple Best in Show and Group

winner, Ch. Norvic's Razzle Dazzle – so aptly named!

In Kansas Laura Purnell, Tomaura, was making people take notice with two commanding stud dogs. First was Ch. Loftis Reenie (from Reenroy lines) with twenty-seven Champion offspring. These included Ch. Tomaura's Moonlight Sonata, the sire of Ch. Devon's Puff and Stuff. The second was Aust. Am. Ch. Leander Snow Star (a Mr Beau Monde grandson) with thirty-four Champions. 'Simon', as he was known, was imported from Australia. A multiple Best in Show winner in both countries he gained lasting recognition here in the US as a highly successful producer, number five on the list of top sires. Mrs Purnell has a line of consistent quality and is the breeder of sixty-two Champions.

In the state of Georgia, Ann Hearn, Jalwin, now an AKC judge of Terrier and Non Sporting breeds, could justifiably boast of Ch. Jalwin Panache of Winmar. 'Boni' is tied for third in the ranking of top producing bitches with fourteen Champions. She was bred to Am. Can. Ch. Diandee Masterpiece from the Diandee Kennel of John and Clover Allen (now also AKC judges of Non Sporting and Toy breeds). This breeding produced Ch. Jalwin Just A Jiffy who would become the mainstay of the noted Paw Mark line. Mr and Mrs Allen also owned Am. Can. Ch. Teeny Teepee's Chief of Diandee. 'Teddy' is currently the No 3 top producing sire with thirty-eight Champions to his credit.

CONSISTENT BREEDING TYPE

An interesting observation at this juncture: The number one and number two top producing sires, Ch. Chaminade Mr Beau Monde and Ch. Vogelflight's Music Man, are father and son. The number three and four top producing sires, Ch. Teeny Teepee's Chief of Diandee and Ch. Beau Monde the Huckster, are also father and son, while number one and four, Mr Beau Monde and Huckster, are grandfather and grandson. Consistent breed type was being established on national level.

Paw Mark, the kennel prefix of

Am. Ch. Crockerly Beau Monde Elipse: National Specialty Show winner and number one Bichon in 1980. Bred by Rosmarie Blood, owned by Nancy Shapland.

Am. Ch Jalwin's Just Jiffy: The 1982 National Specialty Show winner. Foundation dog of the Pawmark Bichons of Pauline Schultz. Bred by Ann Hearn (Jalwin).

Am. Ch. Paw Mark's Talk Of The Town: No 1 Bichon in 1984 with multiple BISs and Group wins. Bred and shown by owner Pauline Schultz.

Pauline Schultz of North Carolina, has become a familiar name on the winners list with sixty Champions to her credit. She acquired Ch. Jalwin's Just A Jiffy who became the 1982 National Specialty winner in addition to his six all-breed Best in Shows and multiple Group wins. Every dog carrying the Paw Mark prefix has 'Jiffy' in his pedigree. He sired twenty-two Champions which included Ch. Paw Mark's Talk of the Town. 'Gabby' was the number one Bichon in 1984 with nine Best in Shows, thirty-five Group firsts and multiple placements and he retained the record of the top winning owner-handled Bichon for thirteen years. In addition, he was a top producer with twenty-six Champion offspring. Mrs Schultz and her daughter Dedee Pierce have had on-going success as owner-handlers of the Paw Mark dogs and others coming from this line.

Margaret Britton and Mary Spruiel, Bererton, a mother and daughter team from Alabama, used both Jiffy and Gabby extensively in their breeding programmes with great success, as proven by their owner-handled forty Champions. Paw Mark and Bererton have continued their association. Paw Mark also aligned with the P-Con

Bichons of the ladies from Utah, Connie Armitage, Paula Ryan and Ramona Lower. This is another combination of bloodlines that has produced consistent quality, for example Ch. Paw Mark P-Con Everybody Duck. He is a sound, elegant dog with the marvellous 'call' name of Quackers and is the sire of Ch. Paw Mark's Fire and Ice, one of the top Bichons at the time of writing.

OWNER AND ARTIST
In the late 1960s and early 1970s Dr Donald and Rolande Lloyd began breeding the soon to be well-known L'Havre Joyeux Bichons. Their dogs were owner-handled successfully and always presented beautifully. They worked with other eastern breeders, a

Am. Ch. Camelot's Brassy Nickel, CDX: Winner of the 1984 National Specialty Show and Non-Sporting Group winner of the AKC Centennial. Breeder/Owner: Pam Goldman.

highlight being their Ch. L'Havre Joyeux Desi bred to Ch. Parfait Apple Crunch. This produced Ch. Parfait Coming Home, ultimately the sire of twenty-six Champions. An interesting aside regarding Rolande Lloyd: from the early days she had shown great talent as an artist and her whimsical Bichon drawings charmed everyone. In the early 1980s she began working in ceramics. Now, for many years, her Bichon statues, depicting the breed at all ages and engaged in all manner of happy activities, have delighted Bichon owners everywhere. She has captured the mood and spirit of this breed as few have ever done.

Joanne Spilman, Parfait, began her breeding programme in the late 1970s. It went into high gear with the advent of Ch. Parfait Coming Home and his succession of top producing and winning Champions. Ch. Parfait Hellsapopin of Druid (co-owned with Betty Keatley, L. Kildruf and T. Lao) was the National Specialty winner in 1988, only the third Bichon bitch to win this event.

Betty Keatley and Betsy Schley, Druid, chose a more restricted direction for their breeding programme and did not go out of their own line to any great extent – but with a notable exception, a breeding to Ch. Parfait Coming Home. There was consistency in their interpretation of breed type and style. Success was obviously forthcoming as seventy-four Champions

143

Am. Ch. Devon Puff And Stuff: Winner of the 1985 and 1986 National Specialties. Top winning Bichon in the US from 1885 to 1998. Breeder/Owner Nancy Shapland. The ultimate show dog.

were the result! Druid Bichons have been winning since the 1970s.

GREAT BREED TYPES

Jane Lagemann, Pere Jacques, of North Carolina, also bred to Ch. Parfait Coming Home and produced Ch. Pere Jacques Sampson d'Parfait. Sampson is elegant, sound, of gorgeous breed type and has produced over twenty Champions. He is very tightly bred and thus has been especially effective when introduced as an outcross into other bloodlines.

Lois Morrow, Chamour, of California, acquired her first Bichon in 1973 but it was obtaining Ch. Chaminade Tempo in 1974 that intensified her interest. While he was a multiple Group winner, Tempo made his mark through his progeny. A Tempo half-brother and sister pair, owned by Dorothy Spear, D'Shar, produced Ch. D'Shar's Rendezvous du Chamour. Mrs Morrow took over this youngster. He won twenty-two all-breed Group Firsts, but his Best of Breed and Group Fourth at the Westminster Kennel Club in 1982 was the highlight. 'Rhoni' was bred to Canadian breeder Dale Hunter's, Craigdale, Ch. Wicked Music of Craigdale. The result was Ch. Craigdale's Ole Rhondi – eight Best-in-Shows, sixty-one Group Firsts and No 1 Bichon in 1983. He was always the showman but is especially remembered for his extraordinary breed type.

Ole was bred to Ch. Chamour Finale (from Mr Beau Monde's 'final' litter!). Am. Mex. Int. Ch. Chaminade Le Blanc Chamour was a result. 'Beemer' won thirteen Best in Shows, eighty-five Group Firsts and two National Specialties, 1989 and 1990. He also won Best of Breed at Westminster and in 1990 became the first male Bichon to win the Non-Sporting Group at that show. Beemer produced Ch. Chaminade Larkshire Lafitte. J.P. won forty-nine Best-in-Shows, two hundred and three Group Firsts and three National Specialties, 1992 and 1993. In May of 1998, years after his official show career had ended, he came from the Veterans Class at the age of eight and won his

Am. Ch. Craigdale's Ole Rhondi: Top Bichon and No 3 Non Sporting dog for 1983. Bred by Dale Hunter. Owned by Lois Morrow (Chamour). Recognized as a fine example of masculine breed type and expression

third National Specialty Show, the first ever won from that class. 'J.P.' always had the reputation of being the consummate showman who never gave less than 100 per cent. The Veteran did so that day. An interesting observation: the four above-mentioned dogs, Rhondi, Ole, Beemer and J.P. (father, son, grandson and great-grandson), all won the Breed and either won or were placed in the Group at Westminster. The breeders are very proud.

Ch. Alpenglow Ashley du Chamour was shown by Mrs Morrow in the interim between Ole and Beemer. He won the National Specialty in 1989 and went on to be the top Bichon and top Non-Sporting dog in 1989. In addition Ashley was an outstanding producer, with twenty-one Champions to his credit, which include several Chaminade Chamour offspring who successfully carry on the line. Barbara Stubbs, Chaminade, and Lois Morrow, Chamour, ultimately combined their breeding programmes, thus using a joint prefix. They have bred eighty-one and forty-six Champions respectively.

Some additional East Coast breeders and their dogs have made an impact in the records books. Ellen Charles, Hillwood, was the breeder of Ch. Hillwood's Brass Band, an outstanding multiple Best in Show and Group winner and the 1983 National Specialty winner. He became the sire of Pam Goldman's, Camelot, Ch. Camelot's Brassy Nickel CD, another multiple Best in Show and Group winner. In 1984 'Nickey' followed in his father's footsteps and won the National Specialty, the first father and son to do so. Nickey produced Ch. Unicorn Nickoles Nickelbee who was the top Bichon for 1987 – an extremely dominant trio. Nickey also became an wonderful Obedience Bichon to the delight of his owner. Mrs Goldman is now an AKC judge for Bichons.

Another mother-daughter combination, Estelle and Wendy Kellerman of New York, Windstar, have been involved in the breed since the early 1970s. They have campaigned

Am. Ch. Scamper Gatlock Of Druid: A Specialty Best in Show and Group winner 1984. Breeder/ owner Betty Keatley and Laura Fox. Shown by Laura Fox, who gained recognition and admiration as head of the US Bichon Rescue Program for twelve years.

Am. Ch. Parfait Vision Of Love: A fine example of the beautiful breed type for which the Parfait line is noted. Bred by Joanne Spilman and Betty Keatley (Druid).

Am. Ch. Pere Jacques Samson D'Parfait: An outstanding sire whose offspring consistently inherit his exceptional quality. Bred and owned by Jane B. Lagemann.

many of their own thirty-seven Champions during the years plus a number of the Robert Koeppel's Calandra Bichons mentioned earlier. A second mother-daughter team has been Doris and Maggie Hyde, Dove-Cote, of New England, who also have been active since the early 1970s. Ch. Dove-Cote's Poise N Ivory has tied for the third position of top producing dams

Am. Ch. Dove -Cote's Mr Magoo and Am. Ch. Dove-Cote's Poise N Ivory: This beautiful duo has produced eleven Champions! Pictured with breeder/owner Doris Hyde.

LIKE FATHER LIKE SON

In the mid-eighties Ch. Montravia Jazz M'Tazz was imported from England by Roy Copeland, Sumarco, Ellen Roberts and Jacqui Kartanos. Razzle made enormous contributions to the breeding programmes of that era and produced an outstanding son, Ch. Sumarco Alafee Top Gun who followed suit. Father and son had twenty-seven and twenty-six Champions respectively, a superb record, of course, but their impact went beyond mere numbers and was an example of the success of introducing bloodlines from out of the country.

Karla Matlock of Arizona, De Ja Vu, became well-known in the 1980s. She has introduced stud dogs from other lines into her breeding programme with obvious success as she has bred seventy-two Champions. Judy McNamara and Jody Collier, Kingscross, have made a significant contribution in the Oklahoma area, especially in conjunction with Jacqueline Fein, Sashay, of Texas. Their Ch. Kings Cross Mister Sashay has been a highly successful 'specials' dog in recent years. Ms McNamara is the Bichon Frisé Club of America's delegate to the American Kennel Club and as such represents the club at AKC Delegate meetings generally held in New York.

with fourteen Champions, while Ch. Dove-Cote's Mr Magoo is the fifth ranked producing sire with thirty-three. The combination of these two Bichons has consistently produced lovely breed type. A third breeder who came into Bichons during this period is Eleanor Grassick of New York, Glenelfred, who was successful on her own (the breeder of forty-eight Champions), but was helpful to others in her area as they began their breeding programmes.

Sandy Orr, Sandon, from Ohio bred many quality Bichons but the father-son duo, Ch. San Don's Friend and Ch. San Don's Friendly Legacy were special. 'Friend' and 'Pal' were highly

Am. Ch. Chaminade Le Blanc Chamour: 1989, 1990 National Specialty Show winner and Group One, Westminster KC 1990. Bred by Lois Morrow and Barbara Stubbs. Owned by Lois Morrow, Carolyn and Richard Vida.

competitive and always major threats at Bichon Specialty shows during their show careers. Pal tied for number ten top producing sire with twenty-five Champion offspring.

Sherry and Chuck Watts, Sheramor, are another line that has been active since the mid-1970s and have been the premier breeders of the Pacific Northwest for a number of years. With their proximity to Canada there has been some interchange, and they have introduced their line into Hawaii with great success. Always willing to help the newcomer, they have been extremely active on both the national and local club levels.

In August of 1998 Ch. Sterling Rumor Has It became the top winning dog in the history of the breed, breaking the twelve-year record of Ch. Devon Puff and Stuff. He was bred by Paul Flores, Sherry Swarts and Nadine Minsky. Rumor has sixty-three Best in

Am. Ch. Chaminade Larkshire Lafitte: Three-time National Specialty Show winner 1992, 1993 & 1998. Group One, Westminister K.C. Bred by Lois Morrow, Barbara Stubbs and Linda Rowe. Owned by Lois Morrow.

Shows. He won the National Specialty show in 1996 and 1997 and was the top Bichon for 1996, 1997 and 1998 and won Group Two at Westminster in 1997 and 1998. The old adage says 'Records are made to be broken,' but this one will be extremely difficult to beat! Always the superb showman, Rumor was presented by Mr Flores with masterful style. He was co-owned by Mr Flores and Meriko Tamaki.

LOOKING TO THE FUTURE

The breeders mentioned above are primarily those who had a serious involvement in Bichons prior to AKC recognition in 1973 or 'joined forces', so to speak, in the decade following that memorable date. With only a few exceptions these individuals continue to make their voices heard. In the latter part of the 1980s and in the 1990s there have been additions to the list of those breeders making substantial contributions. Only time will tell if they will continue be active in the upcoming decade.

From east to west they are: Linda Dickens, Sandcastle; Carol and Michela Konik, Doriann; Mimi Winkler, Judges Choice; Lori and Tracy Kornfeld, Pillowtalk; Kay Hughes, Diamant; Jill Cohen, Seastar; Bill Dreker, Nuage; John and Leanne Wise, Clarion; Barbara Barton, Spellbound; Keith and Sandra Hansen, Saks; and Erayna Beckman, Legend, to mention but a few.

TOP HANDLERS

Many breeders show their own dogs, but others have turned to the professional handler. While often handling all breeds, many professionals have become known for their interest in the Bichons and for their ability to present them with special style. Pauline and Joe Waterman (California) were the

Am. Ch. Gold Coast Saks Jackpot: 1995 National Specialty show winner. Owner, Sandra and Keith Hanson (Saks)

first to become involved, not only as handlers but as successful breeders. Mr Waterman showed the great Ch. Vogelflight's Music Man for his three-year career, Ch. Chaminade Le Blanc Chamour for his show days, plus a consistent run of top Bichons. Michael Kemp (Texas) showed Ch. Devon Puff and Stuff through her record-breaking career, then took Ch. Alpenglow Ashley du Chamour to top Non Sporting dog honors.

Clifford Steele on the East coast carried a father, son, grandson trio (Ch. Hillwood Brass Band, Ch. Camelots' Brassy Nickel and Ch. Nickoles Nickelbee) to years of success. In 1990 Bill McFadden (Northern California) entered the scene. Mr McFadden handled Ch. Chaminade Larkshire Lafitte through Specialties and an all-breed career and continues with outstanding 'specials' dogs. Paul Flores

has bred Bichons for a number of years but has also been a successful professional handler. Ch. Sterling Rumor Has It took those handling talents to the top.

THE BREED'S PROGRESS

Bichon owners have been proud of the progress of the breed since the official recognition twenty-five years ago. There have been no regrets over the decision to gain placement in the Non Sporting Group as opposed to the Toy Group.

The American perception of the breed was not that of a 'toy' dog. In addition, there was concern that attempts to breed ever smaller dogs to conform to the 'toy' concept could bring about a reduction in quality. The Bichon has been extraordinarily successful in competition on the all-breed level on a national basis, in addition to becoming a popular companion dog. This is

Am. Ch. Beau Monde Miss Chaminade. From his final litter, 'Christy' is the last known living offspring of the great Mr Beau Monde.

Am. Ch. Paw Mark's Fire And Ice: One of the top Bichons shown during the 1997-98 period with multiple BIS and Specialty wins. Owners Pauline Schultz and Cecilia Ruggles.

doubtless as a result of the breed's temperament and size and because of that enormously appealing quality the breed universally exhibits.

The advancement of the breed can be credited in large part to the work of the Bichon Frisé Club of America, Inc., the parent club, and the local Bichon clubs spread geographically throughout the United States. The BFCA holds an annual Specialty show, hosted by a different local club each year and, occasionally, by the parent club itself. This is a major event for national Bichon owners, with old friends meeting once again, the opportunity to see new youngsters coming up, and the excitement of the final competition for the top dog.

BFCA oversees a major National Rescue Programme, which has been chaired by Laura Fox of Wisconsin (Foxlaur) for the past twelve years. Doing what is often a heart-wrenching job, this dedicated lady has organized referral services throughout the country and, with her large team of workers, has placed an incredible number of abandoned dogs, or dogs the owners cannot, or will not, continue to keep. The parent club also supervises a Health and Education Programme currently chaired by Anne Jones (Enjoue) of Georgia. An educational seminar is held in conjunction with every annual National Specialty. Emphasis is put on X-ray for OFA (Orthopedic Foundation of America) to certify absence of hip dysplasia and on CERF (Canine Eye Research Foundation) to certify absence of juvenile cataracts. The American Kennel Club considers both important enough in all breeds to now include the certification numbers on registration papers. Microchips and/or a tattoo is encouraged for identification purposes. An educational pamphlet is enclosed with every National Bulletin and special educational mailings are sent to members when appropriate, DNA information currently being one of the hottest topics.

LOCAL CLUBS

The local clubs operate in much the same manner as the national, but obviously on a lesser scale. There are fourteen such clubs today: Southern New England, New York, New Jersey, Chicago, St. Louis, Minnesota, Michigan, Colorado, Dallas, Houston, San Diego, Los Angeles, Northern California and Washington (state). In addition to the 'show' enthusiasts, these clubs enthusiastically welcome all pet owners. Members enjoy social and educational aspects plus assisting with the annual local Specialty shows. 'A Day in the Park' is a popular event for the local groups. All Bichons are invited and innovative events are scheduled so that people and dogs alike spend a marvellous day.

American Bichon owners have participated in the three International Bichon Congresses held thus far, in London, Sydney and Los Angeles. Wonderful friendships have been established on these occasions and everyone looks forward to the next event.

The Bichon Frisé is a real treasure. It delights all Bichon enthusiasts to know our breed has reached the level of recognition and respect it so richly deserves.

12 THE BICHON FRISE IN THE UK

Although many new breeds had been introduced into the UK since the end of the Second World War it was not until 1974 that the Bichon Frisé arrived and became an instant success.

The breed was first brought to the notice of the dog fraternity in a column written by Tom Horner in *Dog World* on May 3rd 1974. Tom, an expert on Terriers and a judge of many breeds, wrote:

"There seems to be no end to the new varieties of dogs which arrive on these shores all eager to join in the fray of breeding and showing after their spell in quarantine. Latest to arrive is the Bichon Frisé, an old favourite on the Continent where several different countries lay claim to its having originated there, and more recently launched with considerable success in America."

Tom went on to briefly mention the breed's background, more or less as I have described in the chapter on the breed's history.

From an article written by Stanley Dangerfield in his "Pets" column in the *Daily Express* on June 1974, I quote the following excerpt as I think I am correct in saying that this was the very first mention of a Bichon ever to appear in the National Press of the UK.

"Another Americanism which may hit us comes in the shape of little white dogs called Bichon Frisé pronounced Bee-shon Free-say and meaning a dear little moppet with curly hair. With dense fluffy coats they look vaguely like cut-down Poodles. Their temperaments are well nigh perfect but unfortunately they need plenty of grooming."

I was pleased to be able to tell Stanley when he returned from the USA that I already owned two charming Bichon Frisé.

THE CARLISE BICHONS
Mr and Mrs Sorstein from the USA

Ra Va's Regal Valor of Reenroy: Sire of the Carlise Bichons.

Above: Aus. Ch. Carlise Cicero of Tresilva, born March 1974. First exhibited in England 1974.

Left: The first English Bichon Champion, Nigel and Ann Worth's Ch. Glenfolly Silver Lady of Sarabande, bred by the late Chris Coley.

came to live in the UK in 1973 bringing with them two American-bred Bichons, a male and a female, Rava's Regal Valor of Reenroy and Jenny Vive de Carlise. The "Carlise" Bichons of Mr and Mrs Sorstein are to be found in the background of the large majority of the original Bichons born in the UK.

When mated, those two Bichons produced two litters, the first in 1974 and the second in March 1975. Carlise Cicero of Tresilva and Carlise Circe of Tresilva born March 3rd 1974 came to join the Tresilva kennels when they were eight weeks old.

From the second litter, born in 1975, Carlise Calypso Orion went to the Leijazulip Kennels of Vera Goold and the late Derek Chiverton, Carlise Colombine joined the Glenfolly Kennels of Chris Coley, and Carlise Canny Caprice went to Betty Mirylees at the Beaupres Kennels. These puppies were the foundation bitches of the Leijazulip, Glenfolly, Tresilva, Ligray and Beaupres kennels.

Ann and Nigel Worth's Ch. Glenfolly Silver Lady of Sarabande was born in 1977. Ann and Nigel had the distinction of owning Silver Lady and exhibiting her to her title. She was the first English Champion, bred by Chris Coley, out of Carlise Colombine. The first English male Champion, Ch. Gosmore Tresilva Zorba, bred by myself, was a grandson of Carlise Circe of Tresilva. Aus. Ch. Carlise Cicero of Tresilva gained his title when exported to Australia to join the kennels of Harry Mackenzie Begg.

During 1974 six Bichons were registered at the Kennel Club. These were Eilish Banks' Cluneen Lejerdell's Tarz Anna, Cluneen Javelot de Wanarbry, my own Aus. Ch. Carlise Cicero of Tresilva, Carlise Circe of Tresilva, the Sorsteins' Jenny Vive de Carlise, and Ra-Vas Regal Valor of Reenroy. These six dogs were the very first Bichons registered at the Kennel Club, that is apart from a pet Bichon registered in 1957. This early registration of a pet Bichon Frisé made it possible for the breed to be accepted for KC registration immediately on its arrival in this country in 1974.

THE FIRST SHOW APPEARANCE

I well remember the great sensation the Bichon caused when seen in the show ring for the first time, at the Hammersmith Open Show in September 1974. I also remember the pleasure and excitement when this puppy, Carlise Cicero of Tresilva, won Best Rare Breed, Best Puppy in Show and Res. Best in Show, judged by Ronnie Irving. His critique makes

Zethus de Chaponay of Tresilva: The first Bichon imported by the author.
Photo: Diane Pearce.

interesting reading: "Res. BIS and BP went to a Bichon, Carlise Cicero of Tresilva. I very much admired this youngster which moved out so well and with such smoothness and drive, good, broad and slightly rounded skull, correct body proportions, with the typical 'overbuilt tendency' which is required of this breed. I was well aware that there would be those who would ask afterwards what I knew about this breed which is so rare in the UK, but having seen quite a large number of them in the USA, I felt confident that this was a good specimen and fitted well into the Breed Standard of the American Kennel Club."

This win was closely followed by Carlisle Cicero of Tresilva going BOB and BPIS at the prestigious South Eastern Counties Toy Dog Society's Show. This was the first Society to schedule separate classes for the Bichon Frisé in the UK.

During 1975 Bianca of Tresilva (Carlisle Cicero of Tresilva ex Carlise Circe of Tresilva) entered the show ring. Bianca became the first Bichon to win a first prize at Crufts; that was in 1976. At that show Bichons were entered in the Any Variety Non-Sporting Classes. These classes were provided for all breeds without an allocation of CCs, such as the Husky, the Hungarian Puli, Belgian Shepherd Dogs, the Maremma, the Estrela Mountain Dog and the Siberian Husky, to name but a few. These were all quite large breeds. The only other Toy breed exhibited in the AVNSC that year was a Chinese Crested.

Seven Bichons were entered. Eilish Banks showed Cluneen Lejerdell Silver Starshine, Cluneen Javelot de Wanarbry and Cluneen Lejerdell's Tarz Anna, who had won a Reserve at Crufts in 1975. I exhibited Zethus de Chaponay of Tresilva, Zena de Chaponay of Tresilva, Bianca of Tresilva and Carlisle Cicero of Tresilva. Zena and Zethus both won a VHC, Cicero won a Res. and Bianca a first. Bianca became the first Bichon to win a Toy Group at any Show.

Until autumn 1975, Cicero, Bianca, Zena, Zethus and Circe, with Eilish Banks' Cluneen Lejerdell's Tarz Anna and Cluneen Javelot de Wanarbry, were the only Bichons exhibited in the UK. All did their fair share of winning, helping in no small way to create the great interest taken in the breed.

THE AMERICAN BICHONS
Not until early 1976 did we have the pleasure of seeing the American Bichons. The breed had captured the interest of John and Wendy Streatfield of the Leander affix, who were already well established as breeders and exhibitors of top winning Poodles. The Streatfields owned their own quarantine kennels, which made it possible for them, with the help of Richard Beauchamp, to import many Bichons from the USA, including bitches in whelp.

The Kennel Club Breed Record Supplement (KCBRS) for December 1975 gives the following details under

Beau Monde The Dove of Leander.
Photo: Michael Trafford.

Import: three Bichons: Beau Monde the Dove of Leander, born December 10th 1975, Beau Monde the Sunflower of Leander, born January 11th 1973 in whelp to C & D Beau Monde the Blizzard, and Beau Monde the Snowdrift of Leander January 2nd 1975. I think the date of birth for the Dove must be incorrect! Snowdrift went to Australia early in 1976 followed by the Dove and Sunflower.

From the mating of Blizzard ex Sunflower a dog called NZ Ch. Leander Beau Monde Snow Puff, owned firstly by Chris Coley and then with Liz Fellowes, left his mark on the breed as the sire of three English Champions. Puff went to be campaigned by Jean Fyfe in New Zealand where he gained his title.

EARLY EXPORTS

In those very early days so many puppies were being exported from this country that an editorial appeared in *Dog World*. It did not have much effect, but its content was so very relevant at that time, as between May 1976 to May 1978 nine adults and 25 puppies were exported to Australia, nine puppies to Sweden, and six to other countries. The editorial headed "FIRST THINGS FIRST" reads:

"When people would rather wear the hat of prolific exporter of dogs than of a successful breeder it is surely time to stop and think. Is the proper aim for breeders to improve their breeds in type and quality, health and freedom from hereditary defects, or is it to fill orders from abroad for stock?.

"In Bichon Frisé, the breed which has been here a very few years, there are already people clamouring for export orders – this in a breed in which the type is far from settled, has no Breed Standard as yet published by the Kennel Club, and very few people interested in the variety with any real background as successful breeders. The few who have such a background are of course extremely concerned as to the future of the breed and for the reputation of British breeders.

"A further worry concerning this new breed is that as a result of the quick impact it has made in the show-ring, dealers are reported to be combing the countries of origin on the Continent for bitches, any sort of bitches as long as they are of an age to be bred from.

"What an outlook for the genuine breeder who hopes to secure good stock and breed something better, as the British so often manage to do. He will, it seems, have to battle his way through a barrage of dealers and wheelers on the lookout for export orders in this breed before moving on to the next likely prospects for a quick profit.

"There has been virtually no time for the genuine breeder to find out what faults and good points his or her stock carries, no time to test the effect of close line-breeding, or indeed for any kind of breeding programme to have been carried out beyond one or two generations.

"As any experienced breeder knows it

takes far longer than this to get to know what breeding stock carries in the way of faults and good points.

"At the moment everyone concerned with the breed is virtually working in the dark – it is certainly no time to be thinking of exporting. When the breed is well established and breeders have found out how their stock breeds on, which strains blend well and which do not then, maybe, is the time to begin to think about exporting.

"Only then can overseas buyers expect to buy reliable stock from Britain."

Unfortunately very few people took any notice of the wise advice. It was therefore not surprising that there were several complaints from overseas buyers.

THE FIRST BREED CLUB

In 1974, with the great interest being taken in this new breed, it was not difficult to obtain the necessary 25 founder members needed to form a breed Club. I was fortunate that when I invited many well-known and highly respected dog fanciers to become founder members, 42 accepted, and nearly all these Founder members were members of the KC .

Sadly many of these members are no longer with us but I would not like them to be forgotten. Among them were Stanley Dangerfield, world-renowned as an expert on all aspects of the dog world, Joe Cartledge, an all-rounder and an expert on Terriers, Reg Gadsden, a great all-rounder, Peggy

Russell-Roberts, an authority on the Papillon, Betty Rawlings famous for the Antarctica Shih Tzu, Graham Newell with the Dokham Tibetan Terriers, and Madeline Harper, an authority on King Charles Spaniels. These seven people were all very experienced breeders and judges. They were of the greatest assistance to me who, at that time, knew little of the whys and wherefores of establishing a breed or the many difficulties I would encounter when endeavouring to form a club for a new and very popular breed.

Many of the Founder members are still very active in dogs today. Ferelith Somerfield has been Patron of the Club since its inception. Of the original exhibitors twenty years ago, only five are still active in the breed today. They are Vera Goold, Leijazulip, Paddy Holbrook O'Hara, Appleacres, Ivy Colvin and her daughter Anthea Marsh, Vythea, and myself, Tresilva.

I suppose the founding of any new club runs into difficulty. This was certainly very true of the first meetings I organised for the foundation of the future Bichon Frisé Club of GB. However with the help of Ken Rawlings as Chairman we held our inaugural meeting at Caxton Hall in April 1976. At that time the Club could only be considered a private club.

In spite of many applications I made to the Kennel Club from July 1974 onwards, it was not until July 1977 that the Kennel Club granted the Club full recognition and we officially became the Bichon Frisé Club of Great Britain, entitled to hold our own shows and events.

THE FIRST BICHON SHOW

The Club held its first Open show in January 1978. This show drew a large entry of 77 dogs with 128 entries, judged by the late Miss Graham-Weall, MBE. As this show was held three years before the breed was awarded CCs, several Bichons at that time would, if CCs had been on offer during the those early years, have gained the title of Champion.

Entered in the Puppy bitch class, winning a first, was Mr and Mrs Worth's Ch. Glenfolly Silver Lady of

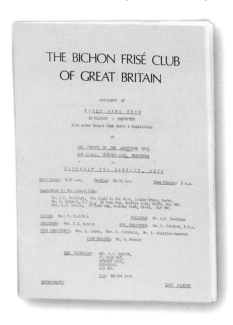

Catalogue of the Club's first Open Show 1977.

Sarabande, produced from a mating between NZ Ch. Leander Beau Monde Snow Puff and Carlise Colombine, bred by Chris Coley. At this very first show, Silver Lady went on to win Best Puppy Bitch and Best Bitch in Show.

The Puppy dog class was won by Mrs J. Fender's Ch. Cluneen Jolly Jason of Hunkidori, bred by Eilish Banks, produced by Cluneen Lejerdell Silver Starshine ex Cluneen Lejerdell Tarz Anna. In 1984 Jason became the fifth Bichon in the UK to gain the title of Champion.

Best in Show was awarded to Wendy Streatfield's import, Am. Ch. Vogelflights Choir Boy Of Leander (Am. Ch. Chaminade Mr Beau Monde ex Am. Ch. Vogelflight Diandee Amy Pouf).

Of the 77 dogs at the show, eight were sired by Aust. Ch. Jazz de la Buthiere of Leijazulip, eight sired by Zethus de Chaponay of Tresilva, eight by Cluneen Lejerdell Silver Starshine, and seven by Huntglen Leander Arden. As I organised and ran these first shows the Tresilva Bichons were not exhibited.

Many overseas visitors attended the show – Mr and Mrs Vansteenkiste-Deleu of the Chaponay Kennels, Mrs Berben of Villa Sainval, both from Belgium, the late Mrs J. Cunagonda Koudijs from Holland, Miss N. Glasscock from Australia and Mrs J. Martinsson-Vesa from Sweden, with most of the Founder members, which helped to make the show a very happy

Ch. Gosmore Tresilva Zorba: The first Bichon in the UK to win a CC at Crufts 1980.

occasion, enjoyed by all. I remained Honorary Secretary from the Club's foundation until I resigned in 1980.

The BF Club of GB now runs a Championship show and an Open show every year and has a flourishing membership of approximately 300. With the breed's continuing popularity there are now four breed clubs, all holding their own shows and educational events. Each Club produces its own News Letter and Year Book which are always of interest.

THE CONTINENTAL INFLUENCE
Research into the pedigrees of 120 Champions shows the profound influence the Continental Bichons have had on the breed in the UK, namely Aus. Ch. Jazz de la Buthiere of Leijazulip; his sire Int. Ch. If de la Buthiere of Antarctica, Astor de Villa Sainval of Littlecourt and Zethus de Chaponay of Tresilva.

These four Bichons were closely related. If was a grandson, and Jazz,

Zethus and Astor were all great-grandsons, of Int. Ch. Racha de Villa Sainval (Kwiki of Milton ex Mowglia of Milton).

Cluneen Lejerdell Silver Starshine and Cluneen Lerjerdell Tarzanna, imported from the USA were both bred from Continental blood lines.

The American influence, although not so profound, came from Am. Ch. Vogelflights Choir Boy of Leander, who accompanied the Streatfields to South Africa in 1981. Both Liz Fellowes' Am. Ch. C & D's Starmaker of Leander, and NZ Ch. Leander Beau Monde Snow Puff are in the pedigrees of several English Champion Bichons. Other American Bichons in our pedigrees include Am. Ch. C & D's Prince Charles of Caywood, and Beau Monde the Fan Fare of Leander. All these dogs, both Continental, and American with the Carlise Bichons, all without exception have Milton breeding in the background of their pedigrees.

BREED RECORD HOLDERS
The breed's first record holder 1987, Ch. Ir. Ch. Tiopepi Mad Louie of Pamplona, became the top winning Bichon for three consecutive years. I believe he won at least 24 BOBs, and was the winner of the Toy Group at Crufts 1987. Owned by Michael Coad, Mad Louie, was bred by Clare Coxall, sired by Ch. Montravia Persan Make Mine Mink out of Leijazulip Sabina of Colhamdorn. This dog and bitch were

Michael Coad's Eng. & Ir. Ch. Tiopepi Mad Louie at Pamplona, bred by Clare Coxall, breed record holder with 26 CCs and 24 BOBs.

Ch. Sibon Jasmyn, bred and owned by Marion Binder.

related. Mink was sired by Ken Rawlings' import Int. Ch. If de la Buthiere of Antarctica, and Sabina was sired by Jazz de la Buthiere of Leijazulip. This was quite close line breeding as Jazz was a son of If and the father of Sabina. It is interesting to note that the dam of Mink, Leander Pleasures Persan, was both a granddaughter and a great-granddaughter of the Am. Ch. Chaminade Mr Beau Monde, who still holds the record as the Top Sire in the USA, producing 65 Champions.

The present breed record holder in the UK with 32 CCs, 26 BOBs, 22 Group Wins, Top Dog All Breeds 1990, owned and exhibited by Michael Coad, bred by Marion Binder, is a bitch, Ch. Sibon Fatal Attraction at Pamplona, sired by Pengorse Poldark of Tresilva ex Ch. Sibon Jasmyn. Poldark and Jasmyn were great-grand and great-great-grandchildren of Zethus de Chaponay of Tresilva and Leilah de la Buthiere of Leijazulip.

Am. Ch. C & D's Starmaker and Beau Monde the Ripple of Leander both occur in the fifth generation of Fatal's pedigree.

To digress a little. By the end of 1997, 118 Bichons bred in this country had obtained the title of English Champion. The starting point for 86 of these Champions was Betty Sorstein's Rava's Regal Valor of Reenroy mated to Jenny Vive de Carlise.

Michael Coad's Ch. Sibon Fatal Attraction at Pamplona, bred by Marion Binder. Current breed record holder with 30 CCs and 26 BOBs.

Am. Ch. C & D's Starmaker of Leander, imported by Wendy Streatfield, passed into the ownership of Liz Fellowes.

REGISTRATIONS

KC registrations in 1975 were 27, but by 1980, only five years later, registrations had risen to 477. No other rare imported breed in the UK has ever gained such a rapid rise in popularity as the Bichon Frisé. This popularity has remained and the breed is now the third most popular of all the Toy breeds and is listed in the top 20 of the most popular breeds registered at the Kennel Club. This chapter gives you the history of the Bichon Frisé in the UK as far as I remember it after 24 years in the breed. If I have inadvertently failed to mention any dog or person, I apologise – but it was a long time ago.

13 THE BICHON FRISE WORLDWIDE

CANADA

I am fortunate in owning a copy of the Centennial edition of the *Canadian Kennel Club Book of Dogs* published in 1988. The front cover depicts an adult Bichon, Norma Dirszowsky's Am. Can. Ch. Tondia's Brite Eyes-Bushy Tail, called Bites, with six puppies. As the breed was not recognised in Canada until 1975, this photograph spread over the front and back cover of the CKC's book is surely an indication of the Bichon's quick rise to popularity in that country.

Bites, bred by Nan and Burton Busk of Hayward, USA, was purchased by Norma in 1984. She also purchased Ch. Dauphine de Franbel from Melville Landry, affix Franbel, of Beresford, Canada. Norma campaigned both these Bichons to their titles.

Norma has bred 23 Canadian Champions and three American Champions. Her Normandy kennels also bred Top Obedience Bichon Frisé

in Canada in 1996. It is not surprising that Norma has twice won the Pedigree Breeder of the Year award. Now as the secretary of the BFC of Canada, a

Anne Yocom's Am. Can Ch. Wendar Fly the Flag, born in USA . English Sire and Dam: Eng. Ir. Ch. Tiopepi Mad Louie at Pamplona ex White Spirit at Wendar.
Photo: Linda Lindt.

Kendra James' Am. Can. Ch. Kenningway Fly Like an Eagle, son of Am. Ch. Wendar Fly the Flag.   *Photo: Patty Sosa.*

Debbie McFarlane's Can. Ch. Aspinrock's Dreams of Gold, a Can. Ch. Sulyka Pandora granddaughter.   *Mikron Photos.*

position she has held since 1990, and as the past editor of *The Bichon Banter* from 1985 to 1995, an excellent magazine on the breed, Norma is without doubt dedicated to the welfare of the Canadian Bichons.

Merville Landry researched and published in 1993 a monumental work entitled *The Pedigrees of French and Belgian Bichons Frisé 1920-1970* which contains no less than 300 pedigrees and 374 names of Bichons both registered and unregistered. Not only is this work invaluable when researching pedigrees, it also makes fascinating reading. Recently Melville sold to M. and Mme. Marcel Guillet, in France, Menaud de Franbel, who is now a French Champion.

I have a request from Norma Dirszowsky which I quote verbatim as I think these sentiments are applicable to all countries: "Please ask Mrs Ransom to credit dogs all across Canada, not just in Western provinces. There are some excellent lines and imports in the East which should not be disregarded. It takes more than 'top winning Bichons' to make this breed and not everyone can afford to show. There are other Bichons that deserve recognition." The photographs of other Canadian Bichons of note illustrate the high quality of the Canadian Bichons.

THE CANADIAN BREED STANDARD

The Canadian Standard for the Bichon has a few slight differences from the English Standard. The Canadian Bichon, as in the USA, is in the Non-Sporting Group. The size is stated as not under 9 inches or over 12 inches. Unlike our Standard, shadings of colour in the coat are allowed even when the dog is over 18 months of age.

There is one clause in this Standard, taken from the FCI Standard, which if I had had my way I would have liked included in the British Standard. It reads: "The circumference of the skull equals the height at the withers, which should be approximately 10.5 inches." This clause is in the original FCI standard. It is a very instructive clause, as a narrow skull completely alters the Bichon's head and expression.

I find it difficult to understand why there is no mention that the pads should be black, as pads lacking in pigmentation are, in the UK, considered to be a sign of weak pigmentation.

I do like the inclusion of the clauses listing faults and disqualifications. "FAULTS: Cowhocks, snipy muzzle, poor pigmentation, protruding eyes, yellow eyes, undershot or overshot bite in excess of 1.6mm, corkscrew tail, too short a coat in adult dogs." I assume the 1.6mm refers to the overshot bite, as undershot is undershot, no matter how close the teeth, and should be penalized. "DISQUALIFICATIONS: over 12 inches, under 9 inches, black hair in coat, pink eye rims," I have never seen a black hair or hairs in any completely white-coated dog.

ENGLISH BLOODLINES IN CANADA

I am grateful to Anne Yocom of the YoAnnewyn Bichons for sending me so many attractive photos of Canadian Bichons. I thank the owners for the opportunity to see photos of Bichons of

Kendra James' Can. Ch. Kenningway's Whispering Heights, sire Am. Can. Ch. Wendar Fly the Flag.   Mikron Photos.

Am. Can. Ch. YoAnnewyn's Francesca, daughter of Can. Ch. Sulyka Pandora.
Booth Photography.

Sandra Greenway's Am. Can. Ch. YoAnnewyn's Col. Billericay, sire Eng. Ch. Sulyka Puzzle ex Can. Ch. Sulyka Pandora.
Mikron Photos.

such quality. Anne Yocum's YoAnnewyn kennels have, during the last 10 years, produced 26 Champions and she has herself won the Award for Top Breeder five times out of the six years this award has been on offer.

During 1989 Anne imported from the UK a dog puppy, sired by Ch. Tiopepi Mad Louis at Pamplona. This puppy, Wendar Fly the Flag, called Pilot, certainly made a name for himself, quickly gaining his title. Am. Can. Ch. Wendar Fly the Flag became the top Bichon in 1991 and No 3 Non Sporting in Canada and 1992 he again won Top Bichon, No 2 Non-Sporting and No 10 All-Breeds. He is still the Canadian Breed Record holder as the Winner of 14 BISs. Pilot is one of only two Bichons Frisés to be placed in the Top 10 Dogs All Breeds. During Pilot's show career he broke every record set in Canada and he is the sire of 29 American and Canadian Champions. The name of Am. Can. Ch. Wendar Fly the Flag will be found in many pedigrees of top-winning Bichons both in Canada and America for years to come.

The four generation pedigree of Am. Can. Ch. Wendar Fly the Flag makes interesting reading. There appears to be little connection between the sire and the dam but, if the pedigree is extended, we find the same Continental ancestors occurring many times in the background of both the sire and the dam. There are a few mistakes in this pedigree which, from an historical point of view, are important. Neither Aust. Ch. Jazz de la Buthiere of Leijazulip, Huntglen Leander Arden or Sulyka Pandora gained the title of English Champion; If de la Buthiere of Antarctica was an International Champion.

In 1990 Anne imported from England a bitch in whelp to Ch. Sulyka Puzzle, Sulyka Pandora, from the Sulyka Kennels. She produced four males, and one, YoAnnewyn's Col. Billericay, became top Bichon in 1993 and No 6 Non-Sporting. Another male from this litter sired Am. Can. Ch. Craigdale YoAnnewyn El Toro who won the American Specialty and was No 1 Bichon in 1996.

Sulyka Pandora when mated to Am. Ch. Wimac Hugo Boss of Deja Vu produced Am. Can. Ch. YoAnnewyns Francesca. This bitch in 1994 beat all the big winners of the previous day's Specialty when shown at the Texas National at the age of nine months, gaining her titles as an American and a Canadian Champion in quick succession.

IRELAND

Although the number of Bichons exhibited in this fair isle is fairly small, it is always a pleasure to attend the Irish Shows both in the North and the South. Irish exhibitors are always so friendly – at least I have always found it so on the occasions I have judged at their shows.

Ch. & Ir. Ch. Hunkidori Serendipity of Alareen wining RBIS at the Tralee 21st Int Ch. Dog Show. Owned by Maureen and Alan Miles, bred by J. Fender.

The Irish Bichon exhibitors breed and show some very nice dogs. The show entries are often increased by the English exhibitors who make the long journey by sea and air as they find these shows so enjoyable. The Irish know how to enjoy themselves and Ireland is a lovely country.

The shows in the South of Ireland are judged to the FCI Standard in which Green Stars are awarded. There is only one show in Northern Ireland, the Belfast Championship Show, where CCs are on offer. Judging at this show conforms to the English KC's Standard.

In order to exhibit at the Southern Ireland shows all dogs must be registered with the IKC, as all dogs entering at the UK Shows must be registered with the KC. To win the title of Irish Champion a dog must win no less than 40 Green Star points, and two Green Stars must be won after the age of 10 months.

SWEDEN

The first Bichons in Scandinavia were imported by Jane Martinsson-Vesa in 1976, a dog named Int. Ch. Tresilva Don Azur and a bitch called Sw. Ch. Tresilva Donna Azur, both from the UK. Don Azur became the first Bichon to become a Swedish Nordic and International Champion. Don Azur is in the background of most of the early Swedish Champions. Another Bichon from England imported by Jane Martinsson-Vesa in 1981, Int. Ch. Leijazulip Guillaume, proved a success in the show ring and of great value as a stud dog.

Three Bichons from Northern Ireland: Spelga Button & Bows, 7 years. Aloria Queen of Sorcery at 10 months, and Ir. Ch. Taleeca Fantasy on Ice of Aloria. Owned by Ann Stott.

Int. Ch. Bichonettes Pantomime Nice N'Easy.

Since those early days Bichons from the USA and Australia as well as the UK have helped to establish the breed's progress and success in Sweden. The Bichon has, from the first, enjoyed a certain amount of popularity in this country, registrations are approximately 500 every year and the Swedish Bichon Frisé Club is said to be the largest in the world with 1500 members.

NORWAY
One of the early Bichons in Norway was Int. Ch. Huntglen Nolie, born October 3rd 1980 (Huntglen Jean-Claude ex Huntglen Georgette of Antarctica), who sired the first Norwegian-bred Champion Nor. Ch. Lollipop My Boy.

Six Swedish Champions.

The overall quality of the Norwegian Bichons means that they have, on my many appointments, always been a pleasure to judge.

FINLAND

The KC Breed records show that the first Bichon to be exported from the UK to Finland was a dog, Beaupres Chico (Zethus de Chaponay of Tresilva ex Carlise Canny Caprice of Beaupres), followed by Bichons from several English kennels. The top winning Bichons in 1996 were the bitch Ch. Leeward's Slick Chick, and the dog Ch. Jitterbop Made for Love. During that year the Leeward Kennels had no less than eight Champions and, the Jitterbop Kennels five Champions, in the list of 18 top winning Bichons.

AUSTRALIA AND NEW ZEALAND

It is reasonably safe to say that most of the original Bichons in Australia were from American bloodlines. The majority of the early Bichons exported to Australia from the UK came from the Leander Kennels whose Bichons were from America, either from puppies whelped in quarantine or older stock of Beau Monde, C & D's and Chaminade breeding.

From the first Leander litter, born in quarantine on September 9th 1975, came Leander Arden, NZ Ch. Leander Snow Puff and Leander Snow Carol (C & D Beau Monde the Blizzard ex Am. Ch. C & D Beau Monde

Rudi Van Voorst and Frank Valley's Aus. Ch. Jazz de la Buthiere of Leijazulip, bred by Madame Desfarge imported to the UK by Vera Goold and Derek Chiverton, exported to Australia in 1977.

Sunflower of Leander). Many of these Bichons from American bloodlines, including Aust. Ch. Carlise Cicero of Tresilva, were imported from England into Australia by Harry Mackenzie Begg. Although books and pedigrees often add the title of English Champion to Leander Arden or to NZ Ch. Leander Beau Monde Snow Puff, neither of them won an English title.

By far the most influential Bichon, imported by Rudi Van Voorst and Frank Vallely of the Azara affix, was Aust. Ch. Jazz de la Buthiere of Leijazulip, imported from France into the UK by Vera Goold late in 1975, then exported to Australia in the autumn of 1977. Jazz is often recorded on pedigrees as a French Champion; this is incorrect. Aus. Ch. Jazz was very successful in the Australian show rings. Winner of numerous BOBs and BISs, he also proved a very popular stud dog,

169

Aus. NZ Grand Ch. Shandau Fame Seeker, bred by J.Warman & E.Rennie in New Zealand, a multi BIS winner in Australia and New Zealand.

producing litters of quality and many Australian Champions..

Zipadedoda Kennels of Julia Jeffrey, with Aust. Grand Ch. Zipadedoda Hidden Meaning (Kynismar Hidden Destiny, bred by Myra Atkins, ex Aust. Ch. Zipadedoda Krisy Kringle), in 1994 won Australasia Dog of the Year (all-breeds), the first Toy and the only Bichon ever to win this prestigious award. 'Meaning' was top winning Bichon of the year three times in his career.

The previous year his daughter, Aust. NZ Ch. Zipadedoda Miss D Mena (Aus. Grand Ch. Zipadedoda Hidden Meaning ex Zipadedoda Maiden Heaven), won BIS at Sydney Royal 1996. She is a multiple Group winner and a Toy BIS winner.

A son of Meaning, Aust. Ch. Zettamay Special Meaning, bred and owned by Hazel Chinery, has won BIS at the breed's Speciality Show and BOB at the Sydney Royal. He is also a multiple Group winner.

Another top-winning dog is David Green's Eng. NZ Aust. Grand Ch. Rusmar Magic Rainbow, imported from England, bred by Dawn Russell, and top All Breeds show dog in NSW two years running. Rainbow, with 52 BISs, was the first registered Grand Champion Bichon in Australia. To be awarded the title of Aus. Grand Champion a dog must have won 50 CCs – no mean feat.

Other top winning Bichons are Aust. NZ Ch. Shandau Fame Seeker, handled in Australia by Caroline Lill, and Mark and Denzil Fallon's imports from the

Aus. NZ Ch. Zipadedoda Miss D Mena.

Eng. Aus. Grand Ch. Magic Rainbow, bred and handled in the UK by Dawn Russell, and winning 6 CCs before he left for Australia. Rainbow became a very big winner in NSW, winning Top All Breeds show dog for two years running in Australia and Top Show winner (NZ BIS in Victoria and Best In Group at the Melbourne Royal).

kennels of Liz Fellowes, Aust. Ch. Ligray El Shaddaye at Ahimsa, a multiple Best in Group winner and BIS, and Aust. Ch. Ligray Cashana Goes Ahimsa.

The Tejada Kennels of Gerry Grieg from Victoria has bred/owned many top winning Bichons. Gerry owned Aus. Ch. Dolorado Demis, a son of Aust. Ch. Jazz de la Buthiere of Leijazulip, who sired many Australian Champions, including Aust. Ch. Dunnrhoen Chartres, winner of the Adelaide Royal in 1985. I understand that a recent dog bred by Gerry, Aus. Ch. Tejada Revenge from Hell, is now a BIS winner in Japan.

Wendy and John Hutchison of Melbourne, whose afix Monjoie is well known in the UK, imported in 1984 Eng. Aust. Ch. Leijazulip Jazz of Zudiki, a grandson of Jazz de la Buthiere of Leijazulip, bred by Vera Goold, owned, handled and exported by Jo Brown. Leijazulip Jazz won eight CCs and seven BOBs and was the fifth male Bichon to gain his title in Australia.

Aust. Ch. Azara Ma Belle Ami, winner of many BIS and producer of no less than 14 Australian Champions, and a daughter of the original Jazz, when mated to Leijazulip Jazz produced many winning progeny – line breeding at its best.

Aus. Ch. Kynismar Show Me Heaven, bred and exported by Myra Atkins, now owned by Julia Jeffery in Australia.

APPENDICES

APPENDIX I: GLOSSARY

Achilles tendon	Easily seen in smooth-coated dogs, joins the muscle in the second thigh to the bone below the hock
Albinism	Lack of pigment in skin, hair and eyes
Affix	A registered kennel name used when registering a dog with the national Kennel Club
Almond eye	The eye set in an almond-shaped surround
Anorchid	Male animal without testicles
Anus	Terminal opening of the alimentary canal under the tail
Angulation	Angle formed at a joint, mainly shoulder, stifle and hock
Bad doer	A poor eater
Back	Region from withers to tail
Balance	Correctly proportioned animal, one part in relation to another
Barrel-ribs	Rounded ribs
Bitch	A female dog
Bite	The position of the upper and lower teeth
Brace	A matched pair of dogs
Brisket	The forepart of the body below the chest; the breast bone or sternum
Brood bitch	A bitch used for breeding
Butterfly nose	Parti-colour nose, spotted with flesh colour
Canter	A gentle gallop
Canines	Long pointed teeth, two upper and two lower, next to incisors
Carpals	Wrist bones
Castrate	To remove the testes by surgery
Cat-foot	Short compact paws like a cat's paws
Challenge Certificate	An award by the Kennel Club for the best exhibit in each sex in the breed at a Championship Show which in the opinion of the judge is worthy of the title of Champion (UK)
Champion	See Chapter Six for the ways in which a Champion is made up
China eye	A clear blue eye
Chops	Broad and deep flews
Close-coupled	A dog comparatively short between ribs and pelvis
Coarse	Lacking refinement
Conformation	The structure and form of the dog's framework
Cow-hocks	Hocks turned inwards towards one another

172

Crabbing	Moving sideways with spine not in the line of travel
Croup	The back, from the front of the pelvis to the root of the tail
Cryptorchid	A male with one or both testicles retained in the abdominal cavity
Cull	To eliminate unwanted puppies
Dam	A dog's female parent
Dewclaw	Extra claw on inside of front and back legs; should be removed from the Bichon Frisé
Dewlap	Loose pendulous skin under the throat
Doggy	A masculine bitch
Double coat	Undercoat with a longer top coat
Down face	The muzzle inclining downwards from the skull to nose
Drive	Good thrust of rear quarters
Femur	The bone between hip and stifle
Flews	The fleshy, pendulous upper lip of some dogs
Forearm	Front legs between elbow and wrist
Gestation	The time between conception and birth, usually 59-63 days
Hackney action	The front feet lifted high in walking
Haloes	Dark pigmentation skin surrounding the eyes
Haw	The third eyelid at the inside corner of the eye
Heat	An alternative word for 'season' or 'oestrus'
Height	Usually measured from withers to ground
Hock	The lower joint of the hind legs
Humerus	Bone of the upper arm
In-breeding	The mating of closely related animals
Incisors	Upper and lower front teeth between the canines, six in upper jaw and six in lower
International Champion	A dog that has gained his title in more than one country
Layback	The angle of the shoulder blade compared with the vertical
Leather	The ear flap
Level bite	The upper and lower teeth meeting edge to edge
Line-breeding	The mating of dogs which share a common ancestor
Loaded	Superfluous muscle
Loin	Either side of the vertebral column between last rib and hip bone
Lower thigh	Hindquarters from stifle to hock; second thigh
Maiden	A bitch that has not produced puppies; or in show classification a dog or bitch that has never won a 1st prize
Metatarsals	Bones between the hock joint and the foot
Monorchid	A male animal with only one testicle in the scrotum
Molars	The back teeth: six in the lower jaw and four in the upper
Occiput	The highest point at the rear of the skull
Oestrus	The period of menstrual flow and the time for mating
Out at elbow	Elbows turning out from the body
Overshot	Front teeth [incisors] of the upper jaw overlapping the lower teeth without touching
Pacing	The left foreleg and left hindleg moving together followed by the right foreleg and right hindleg
Pastern	The area between the wrist above and the digits below
Patella	The knee cap; part of the stifle joint
Pigeon-toed	Forefeet inclined inwards
Pigment	Colour of skin
Plume	Long hair hanging from the tail
Prefix	See Affix
Premolar	The teeth between the canines and the molars: eight in the top jaw and eight in the lower jaw

Puppy	A dog up to 12 months of age
Puppy Class	Classes for puppies between 6 and 12 months
Quality	Refinement
Ring tail	Carried up almost in a circle
Roach back	A convex curvature of the back
Scissor bite	Upper teeth closely overlap and touch the lower teeth
Second thigh	The part of the hindquarters from stifle to hock
Sire	A dog's male parent
Slab sided	Flat ribs
Snipy	Muzzle pointed and weak
Spay	To remove surgically the ovaries and uterus to prevent conception
Splayed	Flat feet
Spring	The roundness of ribs
Standard	The official 'word picture' of a breed
Sternum	Breast bone
Stifle	Knee
Stop	Indentation between the eyes
Stud Book	A Kennel Club record of winning dogs, used for breeding purposes
Straight in shoulder	Shoulder blades insufficiently laid back
Thigh	Hindquarters from hip to stifle
Throatiness	An excess of skin under the throat
Topknot	The long hair on the head
Topline	The outline of a dog from withers to tail-set
Toy dog	A small dog, i.e. a lap dog
Tuck-up	An upward curve from rib end to waist
Type	Qualities that distinguish a breed
Undercoat	A dense, soft, short coat concealed by a longer top coat
Undershot	The lower front teeth [incisors] overlapping the front teeth of the upper jaw
Upper arm	The humerus or bone of the foreleg between shoulder blade and forearm
Upright shoulder	Steep in shoulder
Weaving	The crossing of the front or hind legs when in action
Whelp	An unweaned puppy
Withers	The union between the shoulder blade and the thoracic vertebrae located just behind the base of the neck. The height of the dog is measured at this point
Wry mouth	Lower jaw not in line with upper jaw
Zygomatic arch	Bony ridge forming the lower eye socket, giving width to the skull

APPENDIX II: ABBREVIATIONS

AI	Artificial Insemination
AKC	American Kennel Club
ALSH	Annexe Livre Saint-Hubert [third class pedigree] Belgium
Am. Ch.	American Champion
ANKC	Australian National Kennel Club
ARAF	Active Registration Applied For
AOC	Any other colour
Aust. Ch.	Australian Champion
AVNSC	Any variety not separately classified
B	Bitch
Bel. Ch.	Belgian Champion
BFC of GB	Bichon Frisé Club of Great Britain.

BIG	Best in Group
BIS	Best in Show
BISS	Best in Specialty Show [USA]
BOB	Best of Breed
BOS	Best Opposite Sex
BP	Best Puppy
BPIS	Best Puppy in Show
BR	Breeder
BVA	British Veterinary Association
CAC	Certificat d'Aptitude au Championnat de Beauté [FCI]
CACIB	Certificat d'Aptitude au Championnat International de Beauté [FCI]
Can. Ch.	Canadian Champion
CC	Challenge Certificate
CD	Companion Dog
CDX	Companion Dog Excellent
Ch.	Champion
CKC	Canadian Kennel Club
D	Dog [male]
Den. Ch.	Danish [Denmark] Champion
ENCI	Ente Nazionale della Cinofilia Italiana
Eng. Ch.	English Champion
FCI	Fédération Cynologique Internationale
Fin. Ch.	Finnish Champion
Fr. Ch.	French Champion
FT Ch.	Field Trial Champion
GB	Great Britain
IKC	Irish Kennel Club
Int. Ch.	International Champion
Ir. Ch	Irish Champion
JHA	Junior Handling Association
JKC	Jersey Kennel Club
JW	Junior Warrant
JWP	Judges Working Party
KC	Kennel Club
KCJO	Kennel Club Junior Organisation
KCSB	Kennel Club Stud Book
KCBRS	Kennel Club Breed Record Supplement
LKA	Ladies Kennel Association
LOF	Livre des Origines Français [1st class pedigree] France
LOSH	Livre des Origines Saint-Hubert [1st class pedigree] Belgium
Mex. Ch.	Mexican Champion.
Mid-Eastern BFC	Mid-Eastern Bichon Frisé Club
NAF	Name applied for
N & MBFC	Northern and Midland Bichon Frisé Club
Nor.Ch.	Norwegian Champion
NSC	Not Separately Classified
NSW	New South Wales
NZ Ch.	New Zealand Champion
OTCH	Obedience Champion
P	Puppy [a dog under 12 months]
PRA	Progressive Retinal Atrophy
RI	Registre Initial [3rd class pedigree] France
RES. CC	Reserve Challenge Certificate
S	Sieger [German Champion]

SBFBA	Southern Bichon Frisé Breeders Association
SKC	Scottish Kennel Club
Sw. Ch.	Swedish Champion
UK	United Kingdom
TAF	Transfer applied for
WELKS	West of England Ladies Kennel Society
WKC	Welsh Kennel Club
WS	Weltsieger [World Champion, Germany]

APPENDIX III: BIBLIOGRAPHY

Without doubt one of the best sources of learning are the many books written by experts both in the past and in the present, which give information on all aspects of the dog. From these books can be learned the methods used by experienced breeders, judges and handlers for the training and welfare of our dogs.

Although all these books do not deal specifically with the Bichon Frisé, they contain much that is of interest and help when dealing with our canine friends. Unfortunately many of the books listed below are now out of print, and some have become collectors' items, but they can often to be found in the secondhand book shops, and the various book stalls that are usually to be found at the large dog shows.

BOOKS ON USEFUL SUBJECTS

Judging Dogs	R.H.Smyth MRCVS, John Gifford Ltd 1972
The Essential Guide to Judging Dogs	Andrew Brace, Ringpress 1994
Genetics of the Dog	Malcolm B. Willis, Witherby's 1989
The Genetics of the Dog: The Basis of Successful Breeding	Burns & Fraser, Oliver & Boyd 1952, rep 1966.
The Theory and Practice of Breeding to Type	C.J. Davies *Our Dogs*
Practical Dog Breeding & Genetics	E. Franklin. *Popular Dogs* 1961
Dogs & I	Harding Cox, Hutchinson 1920
Conformation of the Dog	R.H.Smythe MRCVS, Faber & Faber 1957
Understanding your Dog	Michael Fox, Coward, McCann & Geoghegan 1972
Dog Steps	R.P.Elliott, Howell, NY 1973.
Dogs in Britian	C.L.Hubbard, Macmillan 1948
Dogs Through History	Maxwell Riddle, Delinger USA 1987
Take Them Round Please	Tom Horner, Faber & Faber 1975
Man Meets Dog	Konrad Lorenz, Methuen & Co 1954
About Our Dogs	A.Croxton Smith, Ward Lock 1931
Training Dogs	Konrad Most, *Popular Dogs*
Canine Terminology	H.A. Spira, Howell, NY 1982

BOOKS ON BICHONS IN PARTICULAR

The Bichon Frisé Handbook	R.Beauchamp, Rothman Publications, Cal. USA 1972
The Bichon Workbook	R. Beauchamp, Rothman Publications, Cal. USA 1975
The Bichon Frisé Today	R.Beauchamp, Rothman Publications, Cal. USA 1982
The Truth about Bichons	R.Beauchamp, The American Cocker Magazine, USA.
The Complete Bichon Frisé	Barbara Stubbs, Howell NY 1990
The Dog Directory Guide to the Bichon Frisé	E. Jackie Ransom, Ryslip Printing, UK 1978
The Bichon Frisé	A Puppy Handbook, E.Jackie Ransom, Ransom, London UK 1995
The Bichon Frisé	E.Jackie Ransom, H.F.&G.Witherby Ltd, London 1990.
The Bichon Frisé	John Hutchinson, J.Hutchinson, Australia 1986
Your Bichon Frisé	Jean Fyffe, Joanne Anderson Pub. New Zealand 1988.
Championship Show Awards 1980-1995	Roy Kelma-Jack, Stroud 1997
Pedigrees of French and Belgian Bichons Frisés (1920-1970)	Melville Landry, Canada 1975